Ghosts of New York: Ten Haunted Places in The Big Apple

Edward Turner

Published by Oliver Lancaster, 2023.

GHOSTS OF NEW YORK: TEN HAUNTED PLACES IN THE BIG APPLE

First edition. July 8, 2023.

ISBN: 979-8223545866

Written by Edward Turner.

Also by Edward Turner

Ghosts of Paris: Ten Haunted Places in the City of Love
Ghosts of London: Ten Haunted Places in The City
Ghosts of New York: Ten Haunted Places in The Big Apple

Ghosts of New York: Ten haunted places in The Big Apple

EDWARD TURNER

Introduction

Chapter 1: The Dakota

Chapter 2: The Morris-Jumel Mansion

Chapter 3: The Merchant's House Museum

GHOSTS OF NEW YORK: TEN HAUNTED PLACES IN THE BIG APPLE

Introduction

A history of New York City

New York City is one of the most iconic cities in the world, with a rich history dating back centuries. From its early days as a Dutch settlement called New Amsterdam to its current status as a global financial and cultural hub, the city has undergone incredible transformations and played a pivotal role in shaping the modern world.

New York City was originally inhabited by the Lenape people, who lived in the area for thousands of years before the arrival of European settlers. The Dutch first established a trading post on the southern tip of Manhattan in 1624, which they called New Amsterdam. The settlement grew slowly at first, but by the mid-17th century, it had become an important centre of trade and commerce.

In 1664, the British seized control of the colony from the Dutch and renamed it New York. The city continued to thrive under British rule, and by the time of the American Revolution, it was the largest city in the colonies. The city played a significant role in the Revolution, with many key battles taking place in and around the city.

After the Revolution, New York City continued to grow and prosper, becoming a major centre of commerce and industry. The opening of the Erie Canal in 1825 further fueled the city's growth, connecting it to the Midwest and making it a hub for shipping and transportation.

The mid-19th century saw a massive wave of immigration to New York City, with millions of people from Europe and elsewhere flocking to the city in search of a better life. The city's population grew rapidly, and with it came incredible cultural and social changes. Immigrants brought with them new languages, religions, and traditions, which helped shape the city into the diverse and vibrant metropolis it is today.

The turn of the 20th century saw New York City become the centre of the world's financial and cultural spheres. Wall Street became the centre of American finance, while the city's art and literary scenes flourished with the rise of the Harlem Renaissance and the emergence of modernist movements like Abstract Expressionism.

New York City played a major role in World War II, with the city's factories producing much of the equipment and material needed for the war effort. The city also served as a major port of embarkation for troops and supplies heading overseas.

The post-war period saw New York City undergo significant changes, with the rise of suburbanization and the decline of the city's manufacturing sector leading to economic and social upheaval. The city also experienced a wave of social and political turmoil in the 1960s and 1970s, with protests, riots, and strikes becoming commonplace.

Despite these challenges, New York City continued to thrive and evolve, with the rise of new industries like finance, technology, and media helping to fuel the city's growth. Today, New York City remains one of the most important cities in the world, with a global influence that extends far beyond its borders.

From its early days as a Dutch trading post to its current status as a global centre of commerce, culture, and innovation, New York City has a long and fascinating history that is still being written today. Whether you're a native New Yorker or a visitor to the city, there's always something new to discover and explore in this iconic metropolis.

The concept of ghosts and hauntings

NEW YORK CITY IS A place of immense history and culture, and as such, it's no surprise that the concept of ghosts and hauntings has taken root in the city's mythology. From the earliest days of the city's history, stories of haunted buildings, mysterious apparitions, and unexplained phenomena have captivated the imaginations of residents and visitors alike.

The concept of ghosts and hauntings is rooted in the belief that the spirits of the dead can linger on in the physical world, either by choice or by circumstance. In many cultures, it is believed that the souls of the deceased may be unable to find peace if they died under violent or traumatic circumstances, or if they were particularly attached to a specific place or object in life.

In New York City, there are many locations that are said to be haunted by the spirits of the dead. Some of the most famous include the Morris-Jumel Mansion, the Merchant's House Museum, and the Dakota Building.

The Morris-Jumel Mansion, located in upper Manhattan, is said to be haunted by the ghost of Eliza Jumel, a prominent socialite who once owned the mansion. According to legend, Jumel's ghost can be seen wandering the halls of the mansion, dressed in the elaborate clothing of her time.

The Merchant's House Museum, located in the East Village, is said to be haunted by the ghost of Gertrude Tredwell, who lived in the house for over 60 years. Visitors to the museum have reported hearing strange noises, feeling sudden chills, and even catching glimpses of Gertrude's ghostly form.

The Dakota Building, located on the Upper West Side, is famous for its association with John Lennon, who was tragically assassinated outside the building in 1980. The building is also said to be haunted by the ghost of a young girl who was killed in an accident on the building's construction site.

While the concept of ghosts and hauntings is often dismissed as mere superstition, it is worth noting that many people have reported experiencing unexplained phenomena in these and other supposedly haunted locations. Whether these experiences are truly the result of supernatural forces or simply the product of overactive imaginations is a matter of debate, but the fact remains that the idea of ghosts and hauntings continues to capture the public imagination.

GHOSTS OF NEW YORK: TEN HAUNTED PLACES IN THE BIG APPLE

It's worth noting that the concept of ghosts and hauntings is not unique to New York City. Similar stories can be found in virtually every culture and every corner of the world. What sets New York apart is the sheer density of its history and the wealth of stories and legends that have accumulated over the centuries.

Whether you're a believer in ghosts and hauntings or not, there's no denying that the stories and legends surrounding these phenomena are a fascinating part of New York City's cultural heritage. From the tales of the Morris-Jumel Mansion to the legends of the Dakota Building, there is no shortage of spooky stories to explore in the Big Apple. So if you're looking for a good scare or simply a chance to immerse yourself in the city's rich history, be sure to check out some of New York's most haunted locations.

The purpose of "Ghosts of New York: Ten Haunted Places in The Big Apple" is to explore the rich history and culture of New York City through the lens of the city's most haunted locations. Each chapter of the book focuses on a different haunted site, delving into its history, its legends, and the strange occurrences that have taken place there.

The book is intended to serve as both a guidebook for those interested in exploring the city's haunted sites and a work of cultural history for those looking to gain a deeper understanding of the city's past. By exploring the stories and legends surrounding each of the ten haunted locations, the book offers readers a unique window into the history and culture of New York City.

At its core, "Ghosts of New York" is about the power of storytelling. Each of the ten chapters tells a different story, weaving together history, myth, and legend in a way that brings the haunted sites to life. Through these stories, readers are able to connect with the city's past in a visceral and emotionally resonant way, gaining a deeper appreciation for the rich tapestry of culture and history that has made New York City the vibrant and dynamic place it is today.

The book is also intended to serve as a tribute to the many people who have called New York City home over the centuries. From the Native American tribes who first inhabited the island of Manhattan to the millions of immigrants who have come to the city in search of a better life, New York City has always been a place of diversity and change. By exploring the city's haunted sites, the book celebrates the lives and stories of those who have gone before us, reminding readers of the countless individuals who have helped to shape the city's unique character.

Ultimately, the purpose of "Ghosts of New York" is to offer readers a unique and engaging perspective on one of the world's most fascinating cities. Whether you're a lifelong New Yorker or a visitor to the city for the first time, this book is sure to captivate your imagination and offer a fresh perspective on the city's rich history and culture. So why not take a journey into the past and explore the haunted sites of New York City for yourself? Who knows what ghosts and legends you might encounter along the way!

Chapter 1: The Dakota

History of The Dakota

The Dakota is one of the most iconic buildings in New York City, famous for its ornate architecture, prestigious residents, and dark history. Built in the late 19th century, the building has played an important role in the city's cultural and social history, serving as the home to some of the most famous and influential figures of the 20th century.

The Dakota was built in 1884 by the architect Henry J. Hardenbergh, who also designed other iconic New York City buildings such as the Plaza Hotel and the Waldorf Astoria. The building was named after the Dakota Territory, which at the time was a relatively new and exotic location, and was meant to evoke a sense of adventure and excitement.

From the beginning, the Dakota was a building of luxury and exclusivity. The apartments were designed to be spacious and elegant, with high ceilings, ornate woodwork, and marble fireplaces. The building was equipped with the latest amenities, including steam heat, electric lighting, and a central vacuum system. The Dakota was also one of the first buildings in the city to have an elevator, a major luxury at the time.

One of the most fascinating aspects of the Dakota's history is its association with some of the most famous and influential people of the 20th century. From the very beginning, the building was home to many of the city's wealthiest and most powerful residents, including businessmen, politicians, and socialites.

Perhaps the most famous resident of the Dakota was John Lennon, the legendary singer and songwriter of the Beatles. Lennon and his wife, Yoko Ono, purchased an apartment in the building in the early 1970s and lived there until Lennon's tragic murder in 1980. The building's association with Lennon has made it a site of pilgrimage for Beatles fans from all over the world.

Other famous residents of the Dakota include actors Lauren Bacall and Roberta Flack, singer Leonard Bernstein, and author Harlan Coben. The building has also been the site of many notable events, including the filming of the classic horror movie "Rosemary's Baby" and the assassination of Italian anarchist Carlo Tresca in 1943.

Despite its prestigious history, the Dakota has also been the site of tragedy and darkness. In addition to Lennon's murder, the building has been the site of several other violent incidents over the years. In 1969, for example, a young actress named Sharon Tate was brutally murdered by members of the Manson Family while staying at a friend's apartment in the building.

Despite its association with darkness and tragedy, however, the Dakota remains one of the most beloved and iconic buildings in New York City. Its ornate architecture, prestigious residents, and rich history have made it a symbol of the city's cultural and social heritage, and it continues to attract visitors and residents alike to this day.

The history of the Dakota is a fascinating and complex tale of luxury, exclusivity, fame, and tragedy. From its origins as a symbol of adventure and excitement to its association with some of the most famous and influential people of the 20th century, the building has played an important role in the city's cultural and social history. Despite the darkness and tragedy that have occurred within its walls, the Dakota remains a beloved and iconic symbol of New York City, a testament to the city's enduring spirit and vitality.

The Ghost of John Lennon

THE DAKOTA, A PRESTIGIOUS apartment building on the Upper West Side of New York City, is perhaps best known for its association with the legendary musician and songwriter John Lennon. Lennon and his wife Yoko Ono owned an apartment in the Dakota from 1973 until his tragic murder in 1980. Since then, there have been numerous reports of sightings and encounters with the ghost of John Lennon within the walls of the Dakota.

According to many residents and visitors of the building, Lennon's ghost is a friendly and benign presence, often appearing in the form of an apparition or a feeling of his presence. Some have reported hearing his music playing faintly in the halls, or sensing his energy in certain parts of the building. Others have reported seeing a figure that they believe to be Lennon, dressed in his signature round glasses and long hair, wandering the halls or sitting in the lobby.

One of the most famous sightings of Lennon's ghost occurred in the apartment that he shared with Yoko Ono. In the early 1980s, a young woman who was renting the apartment claimed to have seen Lennon's ghost sitting at the foot of her bed. According to her account, Lennon appeared to be deep in thought, as if he was composing music or lyrics in his head. When the woman asked Lennon if he was all right, he looked up at her and smiled, then disappeared.

Another reported encounter with Lennon's ghost occurred in the building's ornate lobby, where he has been seen sitting on a bench or wandering the halls. One resident reported feeling a tap on his shoulder while standing in the lobby, and when he turned around, he saw Lennon standing behind him, dressed in his iconic white suit.

Despite the many reports of Lennon's ghost, there are some who remain sceptical of such claims. Some sceptics argue that the sightings are simply the result of people's overactive imaginations or wishful thinking. Others suggest that the ghost stories may be a clever marketing ploy by the Dakota's owners to attract visitors and boost the building's profile.

Despite the sceptics, however, many people continue to believe in the existence of Lennon's ghost and are drawn to the Dakota to experience his presence for themselves. The building has become something of a pilgrimage site for Beatles fans and Lennon enthusiasts from all over the world, who come to pay their respects to the musician and perhaps catch a glimpse of his ghostly presence.

The ghost of John Lennon is a fascinating and enduring legend associated with the Dakota apartment building in New York City. Despite the scepticism of some, the numerous reports of sightings and encounters with Lennon's ghost suggest that his spirit may still be present within the walls of the building. Whether or not one believes in ghosts, the legend of John Lennon's ghost has become an important part of the Dakota's rich cultural and social history, and a testament to the enduring legacy of one of the greatest musicians of all time.

Other reported hauntings

THE DAKOTA, A HISTORIC apartment building located in the Upper West Side of New York City, is known not only for its prestigious architecture and residents, but also for its supposed hauntings. In addition to the famous ghost of John Lennon, there have been numerous reports of other ghostly occurrences within the building. Let's explore some of the other reported hauntings at the Dakota.

One of the most commonly reported ghost sightings at the Dakota is that of a young girl named Dorothy. According to legend, Dorothy was the daughter of a former resident of the building who died tragically in the early 20th century. She has been seen wandering the halls of the Dakota in a white dress, sometimes accompanied by her mother or a nanny. Dorothy's ghost is said to be a friendly presence, often seen smiling or waving at passersby.

Another reported haunting at the Dakota is that of a man in a top hat and tails. According to some accounts, the man appears in the building's elevators, but disappears before reaching his destination. Others have reported seeing him standing in the lobby or walking down the hallways. The identity of this mysterious figure is unknown, but some believe he may be a former resident of the building who passed away and still lingers on as a ghost.

The ghost of a former maintenance worker has also been reported at the Dakota. According to some residents, the maintenance worker was killed in the building's basement during an accident in the early 20th century. His ghost has been seen walking the halls of the basement, dressed in his work clothes and carrying a tool box. Some have reported hearing strange noises or feeling an eerie presence while in the basement, leading them to believe that the maintenance worker's ghost may still be lingering there.

There have also been reports of a ghostly cat that roams the halls of the Dakota. According to legend, the cat belonged to a former resident who died in the building. The cat's ghost has been seen darting around corners and disappearing into walls, or simply sitting and staring at passersby. Some believe that the cat's ghost may be a comforting presence, watching over the building's residents and keeping them safe.

Despite the many reports of hauntings at the Dakota, there are some who remain sceptical of such claims. Some argue that the stories are simply urban legends or the result of overactive imaginations. Others suggest that the building's owners may be perpetuating the ghost stories as a marketing ploy to attract visitors and boost the building's prestige.

Whether or not one believes in ghosts, the reported hauntings at the Dakota have become a part of the building's rich cultural history and lore. They add to the mystique and allure of this iconic building, drawing visitors and residents alike to explore its halls and imagine the many stories and secrets that lie within.

Theories and explanations for the hauntings

THE DAKOTA IS KNOWN for its rich history, beautiful architecture, and rumoured hauntings. Over the years, there have been numerous reports of ghost sightings and unexplained phenomena within the building. While some believe these occurrences are evidence of paranormal activity, others offer more sceptical explanations. Let's explore some of the theories and explanations for the hauntings at the Dakota.

One theory is that the hauntings at the Dakota are the result of the building's age and history. The Dakota was built in the late 19th century, and over the years it has been home to many prominent New Yorkers, including musicians, actors, and politicians. With such a long and varied history, it is not difficult to imagine that the building could have accumulated some residual energy or memories that manifest as ghostly apparitions.

Another theory is that the hauntings at the Dakota are the result of psychological suggestion. According to this theory, people who are already inclined to believe in ghosts may be more likely to interpret strange occurrences within the building as evidence of paranormal activity. In other words, the power of suggestion may be leading people to see or hear things that aren't really there.

There are also those who argue that the hauntings at the Dakota are nothing more than hoaxes or publicity stunts. Some believe that the building's owners or managers may be perpetuating the ghost stories as a way to generate buzz and attract visitors. While there is no concrete evidence to support this theory, it is certainly a possibility.

Another explanation for the hauntings at the Dakota is that they are the result of electromagnetic fields (EMFs). EMFs are invisible energy fields that are created by electronic devices and other sources of energy. Some studies have suggested that exposure to high levels of EMFs can cause hallucinations, headaches, and other physical and psychological symptoms. If the Dakota is home to high levels of EMFs, it is possible that these fields could be causing some of the reported ghost sightings and other unexplained phenomena.

Finally, there are those who believe that the hauntings at the Dakota are the result of actual paranormal activity. According to this theory, the building is home to spirits who have not yet moved on to the afterlife. Whether these spirits are former residents or simply entities that have attached themselves to the building over time, the belief in actual ghosts remains a possibility.

Ultimately, the theories and explanations for the hauntings at the Dakota are varied and often contentious. While some believe that the building is truly haunted, others argue that the reported ghost sightings and other unexplained phenomena can be explained through more rational means. Regardless of one's beliefs, however, there is no denying that the Dakota is a fascinating and mysterious place that continues to capture the imaginations of people from all over the world.

EDWARD TURNER

Chapter 2: The Morris-Jumel Mansion

History of the Morris-Jumel Mansion

The Morris-Jumel Mansion is a historical landmark located in Washington Heights, New York City. It is the oldest house in Manhattan and has played an important role in the history of the city. The mansion was built in 1765 by British Colonel Roger Morris and his American wife Mary Philipse. It was originally known as the Mount Morris Mansion and was built on a hill overlooking the Harlem River.

During the American Revolution, the mansion played a crucial role as a strategic location for both American and British forces. The mansion was used by both sides as a headquarters, and the Battle of Harlem Heights was fought nearby. George Washington stayed at the mansion twice during the war and used it as a headquarters for a short period of time.

After the war, the mansion was sold to Stephen Jumel, a French businessman who had made his fortune in Haiti. Jumel and his wife, Eliza, renovated and expanded the mansion, adding several rooms and modernising the interior. Eliza was known for her lavish parties and hosted many notable figures, including Aaron Burr and Thomas Jefferson.

The mansion continued to change hands throughout the 19th century, and by the early 20th century it had fallen into disrepair. In 1903, the mansion was purchased by the City of New York and turned into a museum. It was later designated a National Historic Landmark in 1961.

Today, the Morris-Jumel Mansion is open to the public as a museum and cultural centre. Visitors can tour the mansion and learn about its rich history, as well as attend events and exhibitions that explore the cultural heritage of the surrounding neighbourhood.

The mansion's architecture is a blend of different styles, reflecting the various changes it has undergone over the years. The original Georgian-style mansion is still visible in the front of the building, while the back features a Federal-style expansion that was added by the Jumels. The interior of the mansion is decorated with period furniture and artwork, giving visitors a glimpse into what life was like in colonial and early 19th century New York.

One of the mansion's most famous features is the Octagon Room, a circular room located on the second floor. The room is decorated with murals painted by Eliza Jumel's niece, and was used as a sitting room and music room during Eliza's time in the mansion. The room is considered one of the finest examples of Federal-style interior design in the country.

Over the years, the Morris-Jumel Mansion has played host to many notable figures, including Aaron Burr, Alexander Hamilton, and even Napoleon Bonaparte's brother, Joseph. It has also been the subject of many ghost stories and paranormal investigations. Some visitors have reported seeing the ghost of

Eliza Jumel, while others have reported strange sounds and sightings in the Octagon Room.

Despite its long and storied history, the Morris-Jumel Mansion remains a vibrant and active cultural centre, serving as a testament to the rich and diverse history of New York City. It is a place where visitors can learn about the city's colonial past, its role in the American Revolution, and its many cultural and artistic contributions throughout the centuries.

The Ghost of Eliza Jumel

THE MORRIS-JUMEL MANSION, located in the Washington Heights neighbourhood of Manhattan, is known for its rich history and stunning architecture. However, it is also infamous for its ghostly residents, the most famous of which is believed to be Eliza Jumel.

Eliza Jumel was the second wife of Stephen Jumel, a wealthy French businessman who purchased the mansion in 1810. Eliza was known for her extravagant parties and lavish lifestyle, and she quickly became a fixture of high society in New York City. However, she was also known for her sharp wit and shrewd business acumen, which earned her many enemies over the years.

After Stephen's death in 1832, Eliza inherited his fortune and continued to live in the mansion. She eventually remarried, to Aaron Burr, the former Vice President of the United States. However, the marriage was short-lived and ended in a bitter divorce. Eliza spent the rest of her life living in the mansion, and she died there in 1865.

Since her death, visitors to the Morris-Jumel Mansion have reported sightings and encounters with Eliza's ghost. Some have reported seeing her wandering the halls of the mansion, while others have reported seeing her in the Octagon Room, a circular room on the second floor that was one of her favourite rooms in the house.

One of the most famous encounters with Eliza's ghost occurred in the 1960s, when a group of musicians who were renting the mansion as a rehearsal space reported hearing strange noises coming from the Octagon Room. When they investigated, they saw a woman who they believed to be Eliza Jumel standing in the centre of the room. The musicians fled the mansion in fear, and the incident has become one of the most well-known ghost stories associated with the Morris-Jumel Mansion.

Over the years, paranormal investigators have conducted numerous investigations of the mansion in an attempt to capture evidence of Eliza's ghost. Some have reported hearing strange noises and voices, while others have captured photographic and video evidence that they believe shows the ghostly presence of Eliza.

While there is no concrete evidence that Eliza Jumel's ghost haunts the Morris-Jumel Mansion, her story and the many reported sightings have made her one of the most famous ghosts in New York City. Her spirit is said to be restless, and many believe that she is still searching for something in the mansion she called home for so many years.

Whether or not you believe in ghosts, the Morris-Jumel Mansion is a fascinating historical landmark with a rich and complex history. The mansion and its ghostly residents continue to captivate visitors from around the world, and they serve as a testament to the enduring legacy of one of New York City's most fascinating families.

Other reported hauntings

WHILE ELIZA JUMEL'S ghost is the most famous of the Morris-Jumel Mansion's reported hauntings, it is by no means the only one. Over the years, visitors to the mansion have reported a wide range of strange and unexplained phenomena, including disembodied voices, footsteps, and objects moving on their own.

One of the most commonly reported hauntings at the Morris-Jumel Mansion is that of a young girl, believed to be the daughter of a former resident of the house. Visitors have reported seeing her playing in the garden or peeking out from behind a corner, only to disappear when approached. Some have also reported hearing her giggling or singing when no one else is around.

Another reported haunting is that of a soldier, believed to be a British officer who was stationed at the mansion during the Revolutionary War. Visitors have reported seeing him walking through the halls in his uniform, or standing at attention in one of the rooms. Some have also reported feeling a sudden drop in temperature when he is near.

In addition to these more well-known hauntings, there have been numerous other reports of strange and unexplained phenomena at the Morris-Jumel Mansion. Some visitors have reported feeling a sense of unease or dread in certain areas of the house, while others have reported smelling strange odours or hearing unexplained noises.

These reports of hauntings and ghostly activity have made the Morris-Jumel Mansion a popular destination for paranormal investigators and ghost hunters. Over the years, numerous investigations have been conducted at the mansion, using everything from EMF detectors to infrared cameras in an attempt to capture evidence of the reported hauntings.

While many of these investigations have yielded interesting results, there is still no concrete proof that the Morris-Jumel Mansion is truly haunted. Sceptics have suggested that many of the reported sightings and experiences may be due to the power of suggestion or the influence of the mansion's rich history and spooky atmosphere.

Regardless of whether or not you believe in ghosts, a visit to the Morris-Jumel Mansion is sure to be an unforgettable experience. The mansion's rich history and stunning architecture make it a must-see destination for anyone interested in New York City's past, and the reported hauntings only add to its mystique and allure. Whether you're a sceptic or a true believer, the Morris-Jumel Mansion is a fascinating destination that is sure to leave a lasting impression.

Theories and explanations for the hauntings

THE REPORTED HAUNTINGS at the Morris-Jumel Mansion have been the subject of much speculation and debate over the years. While some people believe that the mansion is truly haunted by the spirits of former residents and visitors, others are more sceptical, suggesting that the reported phenomena may have more mundane explanations.

One theory that is often put forth to explain the hauntings is that they are the result of residual energy left behind by people who lived or died at the mansion. According to this theory, certain emotional or traumatic events can leave behind an imprint on the environment, which can then be felt or sensed by sensitive individuals. This residual energy could explain the reported sightings of ghostly figures and the strange sensations reported by visitors to the mansion.

Another theory is that the reported hauntings at the Morris-Jumel Mansion are the result of the power of suggestion. The mansion's rich history and spooky atmosphere may make visitors more susceptible to imagining or experiencing supernatural phenomena. In other words, people may be more likely to see or hear something unusual because they are already primed to expect it.

Yet another theory is that the reported hauntings are the result of natural phenomena that have been misinterpreted as supernatural. For example, some of the reported noises or sensations could be the result of the house settling or creaking, while others may be the result of drafts or other environmental factors. Similarly, some of the reported sightings of ghostly figures could be the result of tricks of the light or shadows.

While these theories provide possible explanations for the reported hauntings at the Morris-Jumel Mansion, they are by no means definitive. The truth is, we may never know for sure whether the mansion is truly haunted or not. However, whether you believe in ghosts or not, there is no denying that the mansion is a fascinating and historic destination that has played an important role in New York City's history.

So if you're looking for a spooky and intriguing destination in the heart of New York, why not visit the Morris-Jumel Mansion for yourself? Whether you're a believer or a sceptic, you're sure to have an unforgettable experience exploring this historic and haunted landmark.

GHOSTS OF NEW YORK: TEN HAUNTED PLACES IN THE BIG APPLE

Chapter 3: The Merchant's House Museum

History of the Merchant's House Museum

The Merchant's House Museum, located in Manhattan's East Village, is a unique and historic landmark that offers a fascinating glimpse into New York City's past. The house, which was built in 1832, served as the home of the Tredwell family for almost 100 years and is one of the best-preserved examples of a middle-class home from the mid-19th century.

The Tredwell family was a prosperous and well-respected merchant family, and their home was designed to reflect their status and wealth. The house was built in the Greek Revival style, which was popular in the mid-19th century and characterised by simple, elegant lines and a sense of balance and symmetry. The interior of the house was filled with beautiful furnishings, artwork, and decorations, many of which have been carefully preserved and can still be seen today.

Over the years, the Tredwell family made many changes and additions to the house, including the installation of modern conveniences like gas lighting and indoor plumbing. However, despite these updates, the house retains much of its original character and charm, making it a valuable and unique window into New York City's past.

In 1933, the last surviving member of the Tredwell family, Gertrude Tredwell, passed away, and the house was sold to a real estate developer. Over the next several decades, the house was used for a variety of purposes, including as a dormitory for New York University students and as a location for a film production company. However, in the 1960s, the house was slated for demolition, as the surrounding neighbourhood underwent significant redevelopment.

Fortunately, a group of concerned citizens recognized the historic value of the house and organised it to save it from destruction. The Merchant's House Museum was officially opened in 1936 and has been a popular destination for visitors ever since. Today, the museum offers tours of the house and its grounds, as well as a variety of educational programs and events that showcase the rich history of the Tredwell family and their home.

In addition to its historic significance, the Merchant's House Museum has also become known for its reported hauntings. Over the years, many visitors and staff members have reported experiencing strange phenomena while inside the house, including the sound of footsteps and voices, moving objects, and sightings of ghostly figures. Many of these reported sightings and experiences are believed to be connected to the spirits of the Tredwell family and their servants, who are said to still haunt the house to this day.

Whether you're interested in history, architecture, or the supernatural, the Merchant's House Museum is a must-see destination in New York City. With its rich history, beautiful furnishings, and reported hauntings, this unique and fascinating landmark offers a glimpse into a bygone era and a window into the mysterious world of the paranormal.

The Ghost of Gertrude Tredwell

THE MERCHANT'S HOUSE Museum is not only a historic and beautiful landmark in New York City but it is also known for its reported hauntings. One of the most famous ghosts said to haunt the house is that of Gertrude Tredwell, the last surviving member of the Tredwell family who lived in the house for almost 100 years.

Gertrude Tredwell was born in 1840 and grew up in the Merchant's House with her parents and eight siblings. She was educated at home and enjoyed many of the privileges of her family's wealth and status, including a love of music and art. Gertrude never married and spent most of her life living in the house, caring for her ageing parents and managing the household.

Gertrude was known to be a private and reserved person, and after the death of her parents, she became increasingly reclusive. She spent much of her time in the house, rarely venturing outside, and even refused to install a telephone or modern appliances. When Gertrude passed away in 1933 at the age of 93, she had lived in the house for almost her entire life and was the last surviving member of the Tredwell family.

Despite her reclusive nature in life, Gertrude is said to be a frequent presence in the house in death. Visitors and staff members have reported seeing her ghostly figure walking through the rooms of the house, often dressed in Victorian-era clothing. Some have even reported feeling her presence in the room with them, as if she is still watching over the house and its inhabitants.

One of the most famous reported sightings of Gertrude's ghost occurred in the 1930s, shortly after her death. A group of construction workers was renovating the house, and one day, while they were working in the basement, they reported seeing Gertrude's ghostly figure walking through the room. The workers were so frightened that they immediately fled the house and refused to return.

Over the years, many other visitors and staff members have reported experiencing strange phenomena that they believe to be connected to Gertrude's ghost. Some have heard footsteps and seen doors open and close on their own, while others have reported feeling cold spots or sudden drops in temperature. Many people believe that Gertrude's ghost is still watching over the house, and that she is protective of the Tredwell family's legacy and the house they called home for so many years.

Whether or not you believe in ghosts, the story of Gertrude Tredwell and the Merchant's House Museum is a fascinating and unique part of New York City's history. Whether you're interested in architecture, history, or the supernatural, a visit to the Merchant's House Museum is sure to be an unforgettable experience.

Other reported hauntings

IN ADDITION TO THE ghost of Gertrude Tredwell, there have been several other reported hauntings at the Merchant's House Museum. Visitors and staff have reported seeing apparitions and experiencing strange occurrences throughout the museum.

One of the most commonly reported sightings is that of a man in a top hat and frock coat, who is believed to be Gertrude Tredwell's father, Seabury Tredwell. He is said to appear in the front hall, where he would have greeted visitors during his lifetime. Some have also reported seeing him in the parlour or ascending the stairs to the second floor.

Another reported ghost is that of a servant girl named Bridget Murphy, who worked for the Tredwell family. She is said to appear in the kitchen, where she would have spent much of her time preparing meals and doing laundry. Visitors have reported feeling a sudden drop in temperature or feeling as if they were being watched while in the kitchen.

The third commonly reported ghost is that of a young girl, believed to be one of the Tredwell children who died at a young age. Visitors have reported seeing her in the upstairs bedrooms, playing with toys or looking out the window. Some have also reported hearing the sounds of children laughing and playing, even when no one else is in the room.

There have also been reports of other unexplained phenomena, such as doors opening and closing on their own, footsteps and whispers in empty rooms, and the feeling of being touched or brushed past by an unseen presence. Some visitors have even reported feeling as if they were being pushed or pulled by an invisible force.

These ghostly sightings and experiences have led many to believe that the Merchant's House Museum is one of the most haunted places in New York City. The museum has been featured on several television shows about the paranormal, and ghost hunters and paranormal investigators have conducted investigations and recorded evidence of activity.

Despite the numerous reports of hauntings, there are still sceptics who believe that these experiences can be explained by natural phenomena or psychological factors. However, the stories of the ghosts of the Merchant's House Museum continue to intrigue and fascinate visitors, and the museum remains a popular destination for those interested in the paranormal.

Theories and explanations for the hauntings

THE HAUNTINGS AT THE Merchant's House Museum have fascinated and intrigued visitors for decades. While many believe that the ghostly sightings and experiences are evidence of paranormal activity, others are more sceptical and seek rational explanations for these occurrences.

One theory to explain the hauntings at the Merchant's House Museum is that they are the result of residual energy. According to this theory, when a person experiences a strong emotion or goes through a traumatic event, their energy can become imprinted on the environment. This energy can remain in the location long after the person has passed away, and can manifest as apparitions or other unexplained phenomena.

Another theory is that the hauntings are the result of psychic impressions left behind by the Tredwell family and their servants. This theory suggests that the strong emotions and experiences of the family and their staff have left a psychic imprint on the environment, which can be perceived by those who are sensitive to psychic energy.

Some sceptics suggest that the hauntings at the Merchant's House Museum are the result of suggestibility and psychological factors. They argue that visitors who are aware of the haunted history of the museum may be more likely to experience strange sensations or sightings, due to the power of suggestion. In addition, some visitors may be more likely to interpret mundane occurrences as evidence of paranormal activity, due to a belief in ghosts or a desire to experience something supernatural.

Another explanation for the hauntings at the Merchant's House Museum is that they are the result of natural phenomena or environmental factors. For example, some have suggested that the creaking and groaning sounds heard in the house may be the result of settling and shifting of the building's structure over time. Similarly, the sudden drops in temperature or unusual sensations experienced by visitors may be the result of drafts or changes in air pressure.

Despite the many theories and explanations put forth to explain the hauntings at the Merchant's House Museum, there is still no consensus among experts and enthusiasts. While some continue to believe in the existence of ghosts and paranormal activity, others remain sceptical and seek rational explanations for these phenomena.

Ultimately, the answer to the question of whether or not the Merchant's House Museum is haunted may never be fully resolved. However, the stories and legends surrounding this historic building continue to fascinate and intrigue visitors, and the museum remains a popular destination for those interested in the paranormal. Whether or not there are ghosts lurking within its walls, the Merchant's House Museum is a fascinating and important piece of New York City history, and a testament to the lives and experiences of those who lived there.

Chapter 4: The New Amsterdam Theatre

History of the New Amsterdam Theatre

The New Amsterdam Theatre is a historic Broadway theatre located at 214 West 42nd Street in the heart of Times Square, New York City. It is one of the oldest surviving Broadway theatres, having opened its doors in 1903. The theatre was built by the Shubert brothers, who were among the most prominent theatre owners of their time.

The New Amsterdam Theatre was originally built as a home for the Ziegfeld Follies, a series of popular musical revues that featured lavish costumes, elaborate sets, and beautiful chorus girls. The theatre was designed by the renowned architectural firm of Herts and Tallant, who were known for their work on other Broadway theatres such as the Lyceum and the New Victory.

Over the years, the New Amsterdam Theatre has been home to many successful Broadway shows, including "Funny Girl," "Annie," "The Lion King," and "Aladdin." The theatre has also been featured in many films and television shows, including "Mickey Blue Eyes" and "Enchanted."

In addition to its impressive history as a Broadway theatre, the New Amsterdam Theatre is also known for its many ghostly sightings and strange occurrences. Many people believe that the theatre is haunted by the spirits of its past performers and employees.

One of the most famous ghost stories associated with the New Amsterdam Theatre involves the ghost of a former Ziegfeld Follies dancer named Olive Thomas. Thomas was a popular performer in the early 1900s who tragically died at the age of 25 from an overdose of mercury bichloride. Her death was ruled a suicide, but some believe that it may have been accidental.

According to legend, Olive's ghost has been spotted in the theatre's dressing rooms and on the stage itself. Some people have reported seeing a ghostly figure dressed in a flapper-style costume and carrying a blue bottle, which is believed to be a reference to the poison that she used to end her life.

In addition to Olive Thomas, many other ghosts have been reported at the New Amsterdam Theatre over the years. Some people have reported hearing strange noises and footsteps when no one else is around, while others have claimed to see apparitions of former performers and stagehands.

There are many theories as to why the New Amsterdam Theatre may be haunted. Some believe that the spirits of former performers and employees simply cannot bear to leave the theatre that they loved so much. Others believe that the theatre's long history of tragedy and loss has left an imprint on the building itself.

Despite its reputation as a haunted theatre, the New Amsterdam Theatre remains a beloved and iconic landmark in the heart of Times Square. Whether you believe in ghosts or not, there is no denying the theatre's rich history and cultural significance.

The Ghost of Olive Thomas

THE NEW AMSTERDAM THEATRE, located in the heart of Times Square, is one of the most famous Broadway theatres in New York City. It has a rich history of performances, from the Ziegfeld Follies to Disney's "The Lion King". However, the theatre is also known for being home to several ghostly apparitions, including that of Olive Thomas, a famous silent film star of the 1920s.

Olive Thomas was a beautiful and talented actress, known for her roles in films such as "The Flapper" and "The Painted Lady". She was born in Charleroi, Pennsylvania in 1894 and moved to New York City as a teenager to pursue a career in modelling. Her striking beauty caught the attention of Florenz Ziegfeld, who cast her in his famous Ziegfeld Follies. It was here that she met her future husband, Jack Pickford, the younger brother of film star Mary Pickford.

Despite her success on the stage and screen, Olive struggled with personal demons, including alcoholism and depression. She and Jack had a tumultuous marriage, plagued by infidelity and substance abuse. In 1920, the couple travelled to Paris for a second honeymoon. While there, Olive ingested a lethal dose of mercury bichloride, a common ingredient in medication at the time. She died in a Parisian hospital at the age of 25.

It is said that Olive's ghost haunts the New Amsterdam Theatre, where she performed in the Ziegfeld Follies. Many people have reported seeing her apparition, dressed in a white, 1920s-style gown, wandering the theatre's hallways and dressing rooms. Some have even claimed to see her sitting on the balcony during performances.

One particularly eerie story involves a stagehand who was working alone in the theatre late one night. He reported seeing a young woman in a white dress walking towards him. As she got closer, he realised that it was Olive Thomas. The stagehand was so terrified that he quit his job on the spot and never returned to the theatre again.

Another reported sighting of Olive's ghost occurred during the restoration of the theatre in the 1990s. A worker claimed to have seen her ghostly figure reflected in a mirror while working in the basement. When he turned around, there was no one there.

Despite these sightings, many people question whether or not Olive's ghost actually haunts the New Amsterdam Theatre. Some sceptics argue that the stories are simply the result of overactive imaginations or even publicity stunts. However, others believe that Olive's tragic death and her connection to the theatre make it plausible that her ghost still lingers there.

Regardless of whether or not Olive's ghost is real, her story is a tragic reminder of the dark side of fame and the dangers of substance abuse. It also adds to the rich history and lore of the

New Amsterdam Theatre, making it an even more fascinating destination for theatre fans and ghost hunters alike.

Other reported hauntings

THE NEW AMSTERDAM THEATRE has had a long and storied history, and it should come as no surprise that it is also said to be one of the most haunted places in New York City. In addition to Olive Thomas, there have been numerous reports of other ghostly activity throughout the years.

One of the most frequently reported ghost sightings at the New Amsterdam Theatre is that of a man wearing a top hat and tails. He is believed to be a former stage manager who worked at the theatre during its vaudeville era. According to legend, he died suddenly and unexpectedly in the theatre during a performance, and his ghost has been seen wandering the building ever since.

Another ghostly presence that has been reported at the New Amsterdam Theatre is that of a little girl. She is said to be the spirit of a young girl who died in a fire that broke out at the theatre in the early 20th century. Her ghost has been seen in various parts of the building, including the balcony and the dressing rooms.

In addition to these two well-known ghosts, there have been numerous reports of other strange occurrences at the New Amsterdam Theatre. Some people have reported feeling cold spots or sudden drops in temperature, while others have reported hearing unexplained footsteps or voices.

One particularly eerie story involves a group of actors who were rehearsing for a show at the New Amsterdam Theatre. As they were going through their scenes, they suddenly heard the sound of a baby crying coming from one of the dressing rooms. When they investigated, they found that the room was empty, and there was no explanation for the sound.

Despite all of the ghostly activity at the New Amsterdam Theatre, many people who work there say that they feel a sense of comfort and protection from the spirits. They believe that the ghosts are simply there to watch over the theatre and ensure that it continues to thrive.

Of course, sceptics may argue that all of these reports of ghostly activity are simply the result of overactive imaginations or coincidences. However, for those who believe in the paranormal, the New Amsterdam Theatre is a fascinating and mysterious place that is full of history and intrigue.

Theories and explanations for the hauntings

THE NEW AMSTERDAM THEATRE is known to be one of the most haunted theatres in New York City. There have been many reports of strange occurrences and ghostly sightings throughout the years. Some people even believe that the ghosts of former performers and workers still linger within the walls of the theatre.

One theory as to why the New Amsterdam Theatre may be haunted is because of its rich history. The theatre first opened its doors in 1903 and quickly became a popular venue for Broadway productions. It was a place where some of the greatest performers of the time, such as Al Jolson, performed. The theatre was also known for its opulent architecture and décor, which may have attracted spirits to the building.

One of the most well-known ghosts at the New Amsterdam Theatre is Olive Thomas, a silent film actress from the early 20th century. Olive Thomas was a beautiful and talented actress who starred in several films in the 1910s. She was also a regular performer at the New Amsterdam Theatre. In 1920, at the age of 25, Olive tragically died in Paris from poisoning, which was believed to have been accidental. However, rumours circulated that her husband, Jack Pickford, may have been involved in her death.

Since her death, Olive Thomas has been seen by many people in and around the New Amsterdam Theatre. Some have reported seeing her in her dressing room, while others have seen her on the stage itself. She is said to appear as a beautiful young woman dressed in clothing from the 1920s. Many believe that Olive Thomas is still searching for something, possibly the truth about her death or closure regarding her unfinished career.

There have also been reports of other ghostly sightings at the New Amsterdam Theatre. One of the most common is the appearance of a male spirit in the balcony area. It is believed that this ghost may be a former stagehand who worked at the theatre in the early 20th century. Some people have reported feeling a cold breeze or a sense of unease when they are in this part of the theatre.

Another common sighting is the ghost of a young boy who is believed to have been a performer in the theatre during the early 1900s. He is said to appear on the staircase leading to the balcony, wearing an old-fashioned outfit and carrying a script or sheet music. Some have reported hearing the sound of a young boy's laughter coming from the same area.

There have also been reports of strange occurrences in the basement of the theatre. Some people have reported hearing disembodied voices or footsteps, while others have felt a sense of being watched or followed. The basement is said to have been used as a storage area for props and costumes during the theatre's early years. It is possible that some of the spirits of former workers or performers are still attached to these objects, and that they may be responsible for the paranormal activity in the area.

The New Amsterdam Theatre has a rich history and is home to many ghostly sightings and experiences. While there is no scientific explanation for these occurrences, many people believe that the spirits of former performers and workers still linger within the theatre's walls. Whether or not these hauntings are real, they add to the theatre's mystique and intrigue, making it a popular destination for those interested in the paranormal.

Despite the many reported sightings and experiences, there are still sceptics who believe that the hauntings are nothing more than urban legends or hoaxes. They argue that the reports of ghostly sightings are based on rumours and stories that have been passed down through the years, rather than actual evidence.

However, for those who have experienced these hauntings firsthand, the paranormal activity at the New Amsterdam Theatre is very real. Whether it is the ghost of Olive Thomas or the spirits of former workers and performers, there is something eerie and fascinating about the supernatural occurrences within the theatre.

Perhaps the truth behind these hauntings will never be fully understood. But one thing is certain: the New Amsterdam Theatre will continue to captivate and intrigue those who are interested in the paranormal, making it a unique and unforgettable destination in the heart of New York City.

50

Chapter 5: The Chelsea Hotel

History of the Chelsea Hotel

The Chelsea Hotel is an iconic New York City landmark located in the neighbourhood of Chelsea. Built in 1884, the hotel has a long and storied history that has attracted artists, musicians, writers, and other creative individuals over the years.

The Chelsea Hotel was originally built as a co-op apartment building, but it was later converted into a hotel in 1905. The hotel quickly became known for its bohemian atmosphere and attracted a diverse group of residents, including artists, musicians, writers, and other creative types. Over the years, the hotel became a hub for the city's counterculture movement and a symbol of the bohemian lifestyle.

One of the most notable aspects of the Chelsea Hotel's history is its association with some of the most famous artists of the 20th century. In the 1960s and 1970s, the hotel was home to a number of influential musicians, including Bob Dylan, Janis Joplin, and Leonard Cohen. The hotel was also a favourite of writers, including Jack Kerouac, Allen Ginsberg, and William S. Burroughs, who famously wrote his novel "Naked Lunch" while living at the hotel.

The Chelsea Hotel was also known for its vibrant art scene. The hotel's walls were adorned with works by famous artists, including Salvador Dali and Andy Warhol. The hotel also housed a number of art studios, which were used by artists to create their works. The hotel's reputation as a centre for artistic creativity attracted many aspiring artists to the neighbourhood, making it a hotspot for the city's avant-garde art scene.

Despite its reputation as a hub for creativity, the Chelsea Hotel was also the site of several tragedies over the years. In 1978, Nancy Spungen, the girlfriend of Sex Pistols bassist Sid Vicious, was found dead in their hotel room. Vicious was charged with her murder, but died of a drug overdose before the case went to trial. In 1980, photographer Robert Mapplethorpe died of AIDS-related complications in his room at the hotel. These incidents added to the hotel's aura of mystery and intrigue.

The Chelsea Hotel has also been the subject of several books, films, and songs over the years. In 1967, the hotel was the inspiration for the Leonard Cohen song "Chelsea Hotel #2," which was written about his affair with Janis Joplin. The hotel has also been featured in a number of films, including "Chelsea Girls" by Andy Warhol and "Sid and Nancy" about the tragic relationship between Sid Vicious and Nancy Spungen.

Today, the Chelsea Hotel remains an iconic New York City landmark, although it has undergone many changes over the years. In 2011, the hotel was sold to a real estate developer, who planned to convert it into a luxury condominium building. However, the plans were met with opposition from residents and activists, who wanted to preserve the hotel's historic legacy.

The hotel has since been sold again and is currently undergoing renovations, although its future remains uncertain.

The Chelsea Hotel has a long and storied history that has played an important role in New York City's cultural landscape. From its association with famous artists and musicians to its reputation as a centre for artistic creativity, the hotel has captured the imagination of people from all over the world. Although the hotel has undergone many changes over the years, its legacy as a symbol of the city's bohemian spirit and counterculture movement will always remain intact.

The Ghost of Nancy Spungen

THE CHELSEA HOTEL IN New York City is known for its artistic legacy and its long list of famous residents over the years. However, it is also known for its haunting stories and paranormal activity. One of the most well-known ghosts at the Chelsea Hotel is that of Nancy Spungen, a tragic figure in punk rock history.

Nancy Spungen was born in 1958 in Philadelphia, Pennsylvania. She had a tumultuous upbringing and was diagnosed with schizophrenia at a young age. Despite her struggles, she was determined to become a part of the punk rock scene in the late 1970s. In 1977, she met Sid Vicious, the bassist for the Sex Pistols, and the two began a tumultuous and often violent relationship.

In October 1978, Nancy Spungen was found dead in the bathroom of Room 100 of the Chelsea Hotel. She had been stabbed once in the abdomen, and Sid Vicious was later arrested and charged with her murder. He died of a drug overdose before he could be brought to trial, and the case remains unsolved.

Since her death, there have been numerous reports of Nancy Spungen's ghost haunting the Chelsea Hotel. Guests and staff members have reported seeing her ghostly figure in the hallways and staircases, and some have even claimed to see her in Room 100 where she died.

One of the most well-known sightings of Nancy Spungen's ghost occurred in 2010 when actor Ethan Hawke was staying at the Chelsea Hotel. Hawke reported that he saw Spungen's ghost in his room, wearing a leather jacket and jeans. He described her as looking "like a vampire" and said that she disappeared after he turned on the lights.

Many people believe that Nancy Spungen's ghost is still searching for justice for her untimely death. Some believe that her spirit may be attached to the Chelsea Hotel because it was a place where she felt a sense of belonging and acceptance among the punk rock community.

In addition to Nancy Spungen's ghost, there have been numerous reports of other ghostly sightings and paranormal activity at the Chelsea Hotel. Some guests have reported seeing the ghost of Dylan Thomas, a famous poet who died at the hotel in 1953. Others have reported hearing strange noises and seeing objects move on their own.

One theory as to why the Chelsea Hotel may be haunted is because of its rich history and association with the arts. The hotel has been home to countless artists, musicians, and writers over the years, including Bob Dylan, Leonard Cohen, and Janis Joplin. It is possible that the creative energy and passion of these individuals has left a lingering presence within the walls of the hotel.

Despite its haunted reputation, the Chelsea Hotel remains a popular destination for artists and creative types. While the hotel has undergone some changes in recent years, including a renovation and change of ownership, it still retains much of its historic charm and allure.

Nancy Spungen's ghost is just one of the many haunting stories associated with the Chelsea Hotel. Her tragic death and troubled life have made her a legendary figure in punk rock history, and her ghostly presence at the hotel only adds to its mystique. Whether or not these hauntings are real, they serve as a reminder of the hotel's rich artistic legacy and the many creative individuals who have called it home over the years.

Other reported hauntings

IN ADDITION TO THE ghost of Nancy Spungen, the Chelsea Hotel is said to be home to many other ghostly inhabitants. There have been numerous reports of paranormal activity in the hotel over the years, and many people believe that the spirits of former residents and guests still haunt the building.

One of the most commonly reported ghosts at the Chelsea Hotel is that of writer Dylan Thomas, who stayed at the hotel in 1953. Thomas was a Welsh poet and playwright who is best known for his works "Do not go gentle into that good night" and "Under Milk Wood". He died in 1953 at the age of 39 from alcohol poisoning. Since his death, many people have reported seeing his ghost wandering the halls of the Chelsea Hotel, usually near the room where he stayed.

Another famous resident of the Chelsea Hotel was Sid Vicious, the bassist for the punk band the Sex Pistols. Vicious lived at the hotel with his girlfriend Nancy Spungen, and it was in their room that Spungen was found dead in 1978. Since then, there have been many reports of strange occurrences in the room, including unexplained noises and objects moving on their own. Some people have even claimed to have seen the ghost of Nancy Spungen in the room.

Other reported ghosts at the Chelsea Hotel include those of actress Edie Sedgwick and musician Leonard Cohen. Sedgwick was a model and actress who was known for her association with artist Andy Warhol. She lived at the Chelsea Hotel for a period of time in the 1960s and died in 1971 at the age of 28 from a drug overdose. Many people have reported seeing her ghost in the halls of the hotel, often dressed in the same black and white striped dress she wore in one of Warhol's films.

Leonard Cohen was a Canadian singer-songwriter who stayed at the Chelsea Hotel in the 1960s and 1970s. He wrote his famous song "Chelsea Hotel #2" about a romantic encounter he had with Janis Joplin in one of the hotel's rooms. Cohen passed away in 2016, but many people believe that his spirit still haunts the Chelsea Hotel.

There have also been reports of other ghostly occurrences in the hotel, such as doors opening and closing on their own, strange noises, and objects moving without explanation. Some people have reported feeling a presence in their room, or feeling as though they are being watched. There is even a legend that a ghostly cat roams the halls of the Chelsea Hotel, although no one knows for sure if this is true.

While there is no scientific evidence to support the existence of ghosts, many people believe that the Chelsea Hotel is truly haunted. With so many famous residents and guests over the years, it's not hard to imagine that some of their spirits may have chosen to remain in the building. Whether or not these hauntings are real, they add to the mystique and allure of the Chelsea Hotel, which continues to draw visitors from all over the world.

Theories and explanations for the hauntings

THE CHELSEA HOTEL IS known not only for its rich history and celebrity guests, but also for its reported hauntings. Many people have claimed to have had paranormal experiences at the hotel, leading to various theories and explanations for the hauntings.

One theory is that the hotel's history and the colourful characters who have lived and visited there have left a strong imprint on the building. The Chelsea has been home to many famous artists, writers, and musicians, including Bob Dylan, Patti Smith, and Arthur Miller. It has also been the site of notable events, such as the death of Nancy Spungen and the stabbing of Sid Vicious.

Some people believe that the spirits of these former residents and guests still inhabit the hotel, perhaps unable to move on from their attachment to the building. The hotel's long history and unique atmosphere could also contribute to the paranormal activity reported by guests.

Another theory is that the hotel's architecture and layout may be responsible for the hauntings. The Chelsea Hotel was built in 1884 and has undergone several renovations throughout its history. Some people speculate that these changes may have disrupted the natural energy flow of the building, causing paranormal activity.

Others believe that the hauntings are the result of psychic energy. The hotel has been the site of numerous creative endeavours, including art, music, and writing. The intense emotions and creative energies generated by these activities may have left a psychic imprint on the building, resulting in the reported paranormal activity.

There are also those who believe that the hauntings at the Chelsea Hotel are the result of ley lines or other natural energy sources. Ley lines are said to be powerful channels of energy that crisscross the earth and can affect human behaviour and consciousness. The Chelsea Hotel is located on a ley line, and some people believe that this could be a contributing factor to the paranormal activity reported there.

Despite the various theories and explanations, the hauntings at the Chelsea Hotel remain a mystery. While some people are sceptical of the reported paranormal activity, others swear by their experiences and believe that the hotel is truly haunted.

The Chelsea Hotel's reported hauntings have captured the imaginations of many people over the years. The ghosts of former residents and guests, as well as other unexplained phenomena, have led to various theories and explanations for the hauntings. Whether or not these hauntings are real, they add to the hotel's mystique and contribute to its reputation as a unique and fascinating place to stay.

EDWARD TURNER

Chapter 6: The Bowery Hotel

History of the Bowery Hotel

The Bowery Hotel is a luxury boutique hotel located in the heart of Manhattan's trendy East Village neighbourhood. The hotel was designed by the acclaimed architect Morris Adjmi and opened its doors in 2007. The Bowery Hotel is housed in a landmark building that dates back to the early 1900s, which adds to the hotel's unique charm and character.

The Bowery Hotel is situated on the famous Bowery, which has a rich and fascinating history. The Bowery was once known as a gritty and dangerous neighbourhood that was home to some of New York City's most notorious criminals and gangs. However, in recent years, the Bowery has undergone a dramatic transformation and is now home to some of the city's most fashionable boutiques, restaurants, and nightlife.

The Bowery Hotel's location on this historic street adds to its allure and sense of nostalgia. The hotel's interior design reflects its historical significance, featuring a mix of vintage and modern décor elements. The lobby is adorned with plush leather sofas, antique rugs, and a beautiful fireplace that provides a warm and inviting atmosphere.

The Bowery Hotel has 135 guest rooms, each of which is uniquely decorated with custom-designed furnishings and artwork. The rooms are spacious and comfortable, featuring luxurious amenities such as Frette linens, marble bathrooms, and custom-made bathrobes.

In addition to its stylish accommodations, the Bowery Hotel is also home to several popular dining and drinking establishments. The hotel's restaurant, Gemma, serves Italian-inspired cuisine in a chic and relaxed atmosphere. The hotel's bar, located on the second floor, is a popular destination for locals and tourists alike, serving craft cocktails and small plates.

Overall, the Bowery Hotel is a beautiful and luxurious hotel that combines modern amenities with historic charm. Its location on the Bowery adds to its unique character and makes it a must-visit destination for those looking for a unique and memorable New York City experience.

The Ghost of Clara Bow

THE BOWERY HOTEL IN New York City is known for its luxurious accommodations and celebrity guests, but it's also famous for its reported ghostly activity. Many people believe that the spirit of silent film star Clara Bow haunts the hotel.

Clara Bow, also known as the "It" girl, was a popular actress in the 1920s and 1930s. She was one of Hollywood's biggest stars and was known for her captivating beauty and charisma. She appeared in over 50 films and was the first actress to embody the idea of the modern "flapper" woman.

Clara Bow had a tumultuous personal life, and in the 1930s, she suffered from mental health issues and became reclusive.

She eventually moved to Nevada and lived a quiet life until her death in 1965.

Despite living far away from New York City, some people believe that Clara Bow's spirit is still attached to the Bowery Hotel. This belief stems from the fact that Clara Bow was a frequent guest of the hotel when it was known as the Bowery Savings Bank building.

The Bowery Savings Bank was built in 1893 and was a prominent landmark in the Bowery neighbourhood of Manhattan. The building's grand architecture and imposing presence made it a symbol of financial stability and prosperity. However, in the 1960s, the bank moved to a new location, and the building was eventually converted into the Bowery Hotel.

Since the hotel's opening in 2007, many guests and employees have reported seeing the ghost of Clara Bow. Some have reported seeing a woman in a 1920s-style dress walking through the hotel's hallways or sitting in one of the hotel's bars. Others have reported feeling a strange presence or seeing objects move on their own.

One particularly spooky story involves a guest who reported seeing Clara Bow's face in the mirror while getting ready for bed. The guest turned around, but no one was there. When she turned back to the mirror, Clara Bow's reflection had disappeared.

While the stories of Clara Bow's ghost are intriguing, there is no concrete evidence to prove their authenticity. However, many people believe that the hotel's connection to Clara Bow's past and the building's rich history could explain the reported ghostly sightings.

The Bowery Hotel is not the only haunted location in the area, as the Bowery neighbourhood has a long history of being a haunt for artists, musicians, and other creative types. The area was once home to many speakeasies and music venues, and some people believe that the spirits of former patrons and performers still linger in the neighbourhood.

The Bowery Hotel has a rich history and is known for its luxurious accommodations and celebrity guests. While there is no way to prove the authenticity of the reported ghostly sightings, the stories of Clara Bow's ghost add to the hotel's mystique and appeal. Whether or not you believe in ghosts, the Bowery Hotel is a must-visit destination for anyone interested in New York City's vibrant history and culture.

Other reported hauntings

THE BOWERY HOTEL IS a luxurious hotel located in the heart of Manhattan's Lower East Side. Although it is known for its sophisticated and trendy vibe, it is also rumoured to be home to several ghostly residents. Many guests and staff members have reported eerie experiences and unexplained phenomena throughout the hotel, adding to its mysterious charm.

Apart from the ghost of Clara Bow, the Bowery Hotel is rumoured to be home to several other spirits. One of the most commonly reported hauntings is that of a woman in a flowing white dress who has been seen floating through the hallways and disappearing into walls. Some have described her as being ethereal and beautiful, while others have reported feeling a sense of unease in her presence.

Another ghostly sighting at the Bowery Hotel is that of a young boy who is said to roam the corridors and staircases. He is believed to have died tragically in the hotel in the early 20th century, and his ghostly apparition has been seen by many guests and staff members over the years. Some have reported hearing the sound of his laughter and footsteps echoing through the halls, while others have felt the sensation of being watched or followed.

In addition to these sightings, there have been reports of unexplained noises and disturbances throughout the hotel. Guests have reported hearing disembodied voices, footsteps, and even the sound of furniture being moved in the middle of the night. Some have also reported feeling a sense of pressure on their chests or being held down by an invisible force, which is a common experience in cases of sleep paralysis.

One of the more unusual hauntings at the Bowery Hotel involves the elevators. Many guests have reported experiencing strange and unexplained behaviour from the elevators, such as doors opening and closing on their own or the elevator stopping at random floors. Some have even reported feeling a sense of being trapped in the elevator and being unable to move or call for help.

There have also been reports of strange odours and sudden drops in temperature in various areas of the hotel. These phenomena are often associated with the presence of spirits or other paranormal activity, and they have been reported by several guests and staff members.

So what could be the explanation for these ghostly occurrences at the Bowery Hotel? Some believe that the hotel's history and location may be the cause. The Lower East Side was once a bustling neighbourhood known for its high crime rates, poverty, and gang activity. Many of the buildings in the area, including the Bowery Hotel, have a long and sometimes tragic history, which could explain the presence of spirits.

Others believe that the Bowery Hotel's luxurious and trendy atmosphere may be a factor. Some say that the energy of the hotel's high-end clientele and frequent parties could attract and even create spirits. Still, others believe that the Bowery Hotel's ghostly residents may simply be the remnants of the city's past, holding on to their memories and experiences long after their physical bodies have left.

Whatever the reason may be, the Bowery Hotel remains a popular destination for those seeking a taste of New York's haunted history. Whether you believe in ghosts or not, the hotel's eerie atmosphere and reported hauntings are sure to pique your interest and keep you on your toes during your stay.

Theories and explanations for the hauntings

THE BOWERY HOTEL, LIKE many historic buildings in New York City, is rumoured to be haunted by a variety of spirits. While there is no scientific explanation for the paranormal activity reported in the hotel, there are a number of theories and explanations that attempt to explain the hauntings.

One theory is that the Bowery Hotel's ghosts are the spirits of former guests or employees who have passed away. This could include those who have died in the building or those who simply have a strong attachment to the hotel. In some cases, these spirits may be drawn to the hotel due to their love of the arts or the city of New York itself. Many of the hotel's reported hauntings involve apparitions of people from different time periods, suggesting that the spirits may be from different eras in the hotel's history.

Another theory is that the Bowery Hotel's ghosts are the result of psychic imprints left behind by past events. This theory suggests that strong emotions or traumatic events can leave an imprint on a location, and that these imprints can sometimes be perceived by sensitive individuals. In the case of the Bowery Hotel, this theory could explain why some guests report feeling a sense of unease or discomfort in certain parts of the building. These areas may be associated with past events that have left a psychic imprint.

A related theory is that the Bowery Hotel's ghosts are the result of residual energy from past events. This theory suggests that energy can be transferred and stored in a location, and that this energy can sometimes manifest as paranormal activity. In the case of the Bowery Hotel, this theory could explain why some guests report hearing strange noises or seeing objects move on their own. These occurrences may be the result of energy that has been stored in the building and is now being released.

Finally, some believe that the Bowery Hotel's ghosts are the result of spiritual or supernatural forces. This theory suggests that the hotel may be home to spirits or entities that exist beyond our physical world. These entities may be attracted to the Bowery Hotel for a variety of reasons, such as its history, location, or the people who frequent the building. While this theory is difficult to prove or disprove, it is a common belief among those who have experienced paranormal activity at the hotel.

Regardless of the theories and explanations behind the Bowery Hotel's hauntings, there is no denying the fact that the hotel has a rich and fascinating history. From its days as a popular vaudeville theatre to its more recent incarnation as a luxury hotel, the Bowery Hotel has played an important role in New York City's cultural landscape. Whether or not you believe in ghosts, a stay at the Bowery Hotel is sure to be an unforgettable experience.

GHOSTS OF NEW YORK: TEN HAUNTED PLACES IN THE BIG APPLE

Chapter 7: The Empire State Building

History of the Empire State Building

The Empire State Building is a world-famous landmark in the heart of New York City, standing tall at 1,454 feet (443.2 metres) high. It is one of the most iconic buildings in the world and is known for its impressive architecture and breathtaking views. The history of the Empire State Building is just as fascinating as its structure, and it has played a significant role in the city's development over the years.

Construction of the Empire State Building began in 1930, during the height of the Great Depression. The building was designed by architects William F. Lamb and Shreve, Lamb, and Harmon, who were hired by John J. Raskob, the chairman of the board of the General Motors Corporation. Raskob was inspired to create the building after visiting the Chrysler Building, which had recently been completed and was the tallest building in the world at the time. He wanted the Empire State Building to surpass the Chrysler Building in height and grandeur.

Construction of the building was an enormous undertaking and took over a year to complete. Over 3,000 workers were employed to construct the building, and it cost over $40 million to build. The building was officially opened on May

1, 1931, by President Herbert Hoover, who turned on the building's lights with a remote switch from the White House in Washington, D.C.

The Empire State Building was an instant success and quickly became a symbol of American progress and ingenuity. Its height and grandeur attracted visitors from all over the world, and it was a popular tourist attraction from the start. The building also became a symbol of hope and perseverance during difficult times, such as World War II, when it was lit up in red, white, and blue to show support for the troops.

Over the years, the Empire State Building has undergone several renovations and updates to keep up with modern technology and design. In 1951, a broadcast antenna was added to the top of the building, making it the tallest structure in the world. In 1964, the building was designated a National Historic Landmark, recognizing its significance in American history and architecture.

Today, the Empire State Building is still one of the most popular tourist attractions in New York City, with over 4 million visitors every year. It offers breathtaking views of the city from its observation deck on the 86th floor and the newly renovated 102nd-floor observatory. It also serves as a symbol of American ingenuity and perseverance, reminding us of the incredible feats we are capable of achieving.

The history of the Empire State Building is a testament to the ingenuity and perseverance of the American people. Its construction during the Great Depression was a remarkable achievement, and it has played a significant role in the development of New York City and American culture. Today, it remains a beloved symbol of American progress and serves as a beacon of hope for generations to come.

The Ghost of Elevator Operator

THE EMPIRE STATE BUILDING is one of the most iconic buildings in New York City, known for its stunning Art Deco architecture and sweeping views of the city. However, there is a lesser-known aspect of the building's history: its alleged hauntings. One of the most famous ghost stories associated with the Empire State Building is that of a former elevator operator named George.

According to the story, George was an elevator operator who worked in the Empire State Building in the 1930s. He was known to be a friendly and helpful employee who always greeted visitors with a smile. One day, George was working in the elevator when it malfunctioned and plummeted several floors. George died in the accident, but his spirit allegedly lives on in the building.

There have been numerous reports of George's ghost haunting the Empire State Building over the years. Visitors and employees alike have claimed to see the apparition of a man in an elevator operator's uniform, who they believe to be George. He is said to be a friendly ghost who still greets visitors and helps them find their way around the building.

One of the most famous sightings of George's ghost occurred in the 1980s, when a woman named Elizabeth Martin claimed to have encountered him in an elevator. She said that she had entered the elevator and pressed the button for her floor, but the elevator didn't move. Suddenly, a man appeared beside her and pressed the button for her floor. When she turned to thank him, she realised that he was wearing an old-fashioned elevator operator's uniform. The man then disappeared before her eyes, leaving her alone in the elevator.

Another reported sighting of George's ghost occurred in the 1990s, when a maintenance worker claimed to have seen the ghost in an elevator. He said that the elevator stopped on a floor where no one had requested it, and when the doors opened, he saw the apparition of a man in an elevator operator's uniform. The maintenance worker said that the ghostly figure disappeared as soon as he looked away.

While there is no scientific proof of George's ghost, many people who work in the Empire State Building believe that his spirit still lingers in the building. Some have even claimed to hear his voice in the elevators, offering assistance or directions.

In addition to George's ghost, there have been other reported hauntings in the Empire State Building. Some people have claimed to see the ghost of a woman wearing 1940s clothing wandering the halls. Others have reported feeling a presence in the building's observation deck, which is said to be haunted by a woman who died by suicide by jumping from the top of the building.

So, what could be the explanation for these hauntings? Some believe that the Empire State Building's history and architecture have made it a magnet for paranormal activity. The building was completed in 1931, during a time of great social and economic upheaval in the United States. Many people suffered during the Great Depression, and some may have left an imprint of their emotional energy in the building.

Others believe that the building's unique design may have contributed to its alleged hauntings. The Empire State Building is known for its long, narrow hallways and labyrinthine layout, which could create a sense of disorientation and unease for some visitors. Additionally, the building's iconic Art Deco style, with its bold colours and geometric patterns, may have a psychological effect on people, making them more susceptible to paranormal experiences.

The Empire State Building is not just a beautiful landmark of New York City, but also a place that has captured the imagination of many people who believe in the paranormal. While there is no scientific proof of ghosts, the stories of George and other alleged hauntings in the building continue to intrigue and fascinate visitors.

Other reported hauntings

IN ADDITION TO THE ghost of the elevator operator, there have been several other reported hauntings at the Empire State Building. These hauntings have been reported by employees, visitors, and paranormal investigators, and have added to the building's reputation as a haunted site.

One of the most common hauntings at the Empire State Building is the appearance of a ghostly woman on the observation deck. According to reports, the woman appears to be in her 30s or 40s and is dressed in clothing from the 1940s or 1950s. She is often seen standing near the edge of the observation deck, looking out at the city. Witnesses have reported feeling a cold breeze or a sudden drop in temperature when they are near the woman.

There have also been reports of strange noises coming from the observation deck, such as unexplained footsteps and whispers. Some people have reported feeling as though they are being watched or followed, and have experienced feelings of unease and discomfort.

Another reported haunting at the Empire State Building is the ghost of a construction worker. According to legend, the worker fell to his death during the building's construction in the 1930s. Since then, his ghost has been seen by numerous people in the building's lobby and on the upper floors. Witnesses have reported seeing a transparent figure wearing a hard hat and carrying tools, as if he were still working on the building.

In addition to these hauntings, there have been reports of other unexplained occurrences at the Empire State Building. Some people have reported strange smells and sudden drops in temperature, while others have reported seeing objects move on their own or feeling as though they are being touched by invisible hands.

Despite these reports, there are no official explanations for the hauntings at the Empire State Building. However, some people believe that the building's turbulent past and tragic events have contributed to the paranormal activity. The building has been the site of several tragedies, including the aforementioned elevator accident, as well as several suicides and even a plane crash in 1945.

Additionally, some paranormal investigators believe that the building's unique design and construction may contribute to the hauntings. The Empire State Building was built during a time when many people believed in spiritualism and the idea of communicating with the dead. It's possible that the building's builders incorporated elements of spiritualism into its design, creating an environment that is conducive to paranormal activity.

Others believe that the hauntings at the Empire State Building are simply a result of the building's age and the residual energy that has accumulated over the years. The building has been in operation for over 90 years and has seen millions of visitors come and go. It's possible that the energy from all of these people has created a sort of psychic residue that is responsible for the hauntings.

Despite the many reports of hauntings at the Empire State Building, there are still many sceptics who dismiss these claims as mere superstition. However, for those who have experienced the paranormal activity firsthand, the hauntings are very real and continue to add to the building's mystique and allure.

The Empire State Building is not only a towering symbol of American ingenuity and engineering, but also a place that has captured the imagination of millions of people around the world. Whether it's the ghost of the elevator operator or the mysterious woman on the observation deck, the hauntings at the Empire State Building are just one of the many fascinating aspects of this iconic building's history. Whether you believe in ghosts or not, there's no denying that the Empire State Building is a place that continues to inspire and intrigue people of all ages and backgrounds.

Theories and explanations for the hauntings

THERE ARE MANY THEORIES and explanations for the hauntings at the Empire State Building, ranging from the mundane to the supernatural.

One theory is that the hauntings are simply the result of the building's long and storied history. With its iconic status as one of New York's most recognizable landmarks, the Empire State Building has seen its fair share of triumphs and tragedies over the years. From the construction workers who lost their lives during the building's construction, to the countless visitors who have come and gone through its doors, the building has witnessed a great deal of human history. Some people believe that this accumulated energy has created a sort of residual haunting, where echoes of past events are still felt in the present day.

Others believe that the hauntings are the result of something more sinister. Some paranormal investigators have suggested that the building may be home to one or more malevolent spirits, who are intentionally causing disturbances and making their presence known. These spirits may be the result of tragic events that occurred within the building, such as suicides or accidents, or they may be the result of something more ancient and mysterious.

Still others believe that the hauntings at the Empire State Building are the result of something more scientific. Some researchers have suggested that the building's unique architecture and location may be playing a role in the hauntings. For example, the building's height and shape may be causing unusual air currents that could be responsible for the strange sounds and sensations reported by visitors. Similarly, the building's proximity to other tall buildings and sources of electromagnetic radiation could be causing electromagnetic interference that could be influencing people's perceptions.

Regardless of the explanations for the hauntings, one thing is certain: they have captured the imagination of people around the world. From amateur ghost hunters to seasoned paranormal investigators, the Empire State Building remains a popular destination for those looking to explore the unknown. Whether or not the hauntings are real or simply the result of overactive imaginations, they have become an integral part of the building's mythology and continue to draw visitors from far and wide.

GHOSTS OF NEW YORK: TEN HAUNTED PLACES IN THE BIG APPLE

Chapter 8: The House of Death

<hr>

History of the House of Death

The House of Death, located at 14 West 10th Street in the Greenwich Village neighbourhood of Manhattan, has a dark and mysterious history that has fascinated and spooked New Yorkers for decades. This imposing townhouse has a reputation as one of the most haunted houses in the city, with a long history of supernatural occurrences and tragedies.

The house was built in the 1850s and has a rich architectural history, with elements of the Gothic Revival and Italianate styles. Over the years, it has been home to many notable residents, including writer Mark Twain, actor John Barrymore, and painter John Sloan.

However, the house's most notorious resident was Dr. Joel Stein, who purchased the house in the 1930s and turned it into his medical practice. Stein was a controversial figure who practised unconventional and often dangerous medical techniques, such as using electroshock therapy on his patients. He also had a fascination with the occult and allegedly performed black magic rituals in the house.

It was during Stein's residency that the first reports of hauntings at the House of Death began to surface. Neighbours reported seeing strange lights and hearing eerie sounds coming from the house, and some claimed to have seen ghostly apparitions in the windows.

The house gained even more notoriety in the 1970s, when the author Jan Bryant Bartell moved in with her husband and young daughter. Bartell was a self-proclaimed psychic and occultist who was drawn to the house's dark history. She began to experience strange occurrences, such as objects moving on their own and ghostly apparitions appearing in her dreams.

Bartell's experiences in the House of Death inspired her to write a book, "Spindrift: Spray from a Psychic Sea," which chronicled her encounters with the supernatural. The book became a bestseller and helped to cement the house's reputation as a haunted site.

Since then, numerous other residents and visitors to the House of Death have reported supernatural occurrences. Some have claimed to see ghostly apparitions in the hallways and on the stairs, while others have heard unexplained noises and footsteps. Some have even reported feeling as though they were being touched by invisible hands.

One of the most famous ghostly inhabitants of the House of Death is reportedly a young girl named Jennifer. According to legend, Jennifer was the daughter of a previous resident who died under mysterious circumstances in the house. Her ghost has been seen by many people over the years, and some have claimed to hear her crying or giggling in the halls.

The House of Death has been the subject of numerous investigations by paranormal experts and ghost hunters, who have used equipment such as EMF metres and infrared cameras to try to capture evidence of supernatural activity. Some have claimed to have recorded voices and other phenomena that cannot be explained by natural causes.

Despite the many reports of hauntings and supernatural activity, there are no official explanations for the phenomena at the House of Death. Some believe that the house's dark history and association with the occult have made it a magnet for paranormal activity, while others believe that the reports of hauntings are simply the result of overactive imaginations.

Whatever the cause of the hauntings may be, the House of Death remains a popular destination for ghost hunters, tourists, and paranormal enthusiasts. It has been featured in numerous books, television shows, and movies, and its reputation as a haunted site continues to draw visitors from around the world.

Despite its dark and mysterious history, the House of Death remains a beautiful and fascinating example of 19th-century architecture. Its ornate façade, intricate details, and historical significance make it a unique and valuable part of New York City's architectural heritage.

Today, the House of Death is a private residence and is not open to the public. However, visitors can still admire its exterior and imagine the many stories and secrets that lie within its walls. Whether you believe in ghosts or not, the House of Death is a reminder of the city's rich and colourful history, and a testament to the enduring power of mystery and legend.

The Ghost of Mark Twain

THE HOUSE OF DEATH at 14 West 10th Street in New York City's Greenwich Village is known for its many hauntings and ghostly inhabitants. One of the most famous ghosts associated with the house is none other than the celebrated author Mark Twain, who lived in the house for a brief period in the early 1900s.

Mark Twain, born Samuel Clemens, was a beloved American writer known for his wit, humour, and keen social commentary. He lived in the House of Death from 1900 to 1901 with his family, including his wife Olivia and their two daughters, Clara and Jean.

During his time in the house, Twain reportedly experienced a great deal of personal tragedy. His daughter Jean died in the house from an epileptic seizure, and his wife Olivia died soon after. Twain himself fell ill and was forced to move out of the house due to his poor health.

Since his death in 1910, many people have claimed to have seen the ghost of Mark Twain in the House of Death. According to legend, Twain's ghost appears on the staircase of the house, as well as in the front windows. He is said to be dressed in his trademark white suit and smoking a cigar.

There have been many reports of paranormal activity associated with Twain's ghost, including unexplained noises, cold spots, and even the smell of cigar smoke. Some people have claimed to have seen Twain's ghostly figure standing in the windows of the house, while others have felt his presence on the stairs or in the bedrooms.

One of the most famous stories associated with Twain's ghost occurred in the 1970s, when a young girl who was visiting the house with her family claimed to have seen Twain's ghost in one of the bedrooms. The girl reportedly described the ghost as a "nice old man" who smiled at her before disappearing.

Many paranormal investigators and ghost hunters have visited the House of Death over the years in an attempt to capture evidence of Twain's ghost. Some have claimed to have recorded EVPs (Electronic Voice Phenomena) that they believe are the voice of Twain, while others have reported strange readings on their EMF metres.

Despite the many reports of Twain's ghost and other supernatural activity at the House of Death, there are no official explanations for the phenomena. Some people believe that the house's tragic history and association with the occult have made it a hotbed of paranormal activity, while others believe that the reports of hauntings are simply the result of overactive imaginations.

Regardless of the cause, the ghost of Mark Twain remains one of the most fascinating and enduring legends associated with the House of Death. His ghostly presence serves as a reminder of the house's rich history and the many lives that have been lived and lost within its walls.

Other reported hauntings

WHILE THE GHOST OF Mark Twain is perhaps the most famous haunting associated with the House of Death in Greenwich Village, it is far from the only supernatural occurrence reported at the historic townhouse. Over the years, numerous other residents and visitors to the House of Death have reported experiencing strange and unexplained phenomena, leading many to believe that the house is one of the most haunted places in New York City.

One of the most commonly reported hauntings at the House of Death is the ghost of a woman wearing Victorian-era clothing. According to legend, the woman was a previous resident of the house who died under mysterious circumstances. Her ghost has been seen by numerous people over the years, often appearing as a translucent figure or as a misty apparition. Some have claimed to hear the sound of her footsteps or the rustle of her dress, and a few have even reported feeling a cold breeze or sudden drop in temperature when she is near.

Another famous ghost said to haunt the House of Death is that of a young girl named Jennifer, who reportedly died in the house under mysterious circumstances. Her ghost has been seen by many people over the years, often appearing as a shadowy figure or a misty apparition. Some have claimed to hear the sound of her crying or giggling in the hallways, and a few have reported feeling as though they were being watched or followed.

Yet another reported ghost at the House of Death is that of a former resident named Ms. Spencer, who reportedly died of natural causes in the house. Her ghost has been seen by several people over the years, often appearing as a translucent figure or as a misty apparition. Some have claimed to hear the sound of her voice or the rustle of her clothing, and a few have even reported feeling as though they were being touched by invisible hands.

In addition to these reported hauntings, there have been numerous other unexplained occurrences at the House of Death. Some people have reported strange smells, such as the scent of rotting flesh or decaying flowers, while others have reported sudden drops in temperature or unexplained gusts of wind. Some have claimed to see objects moving on their own or to have heard unexplained noises, such as footsteps, whispers, or laughter.

The House of Death has been the subject of numerous investigations by paranormal experts and ghost hunters, who have used equipment such as EMF metres and infrared cameras to try to capture evidence of supernatural activity. Some have claimed to have recorded voices and other phenomena that cannot be explained by natural causes, while others have been unable to capture any evidence of paranormal activity.

Despite the many reports of hauntings and supernatural occurrences at the House of Death, there are no official explanations for the phenomena. Some believe that the house's dark history and association with the occult have made it a magnet for paranormal activity, while others believe that the reports of hauntings are simply the result of overactive imaginations.

Regardless of the cause of the hauntings, the House of Death remains one of the most fascinating and mysterious places in New York City. Its long and storied history, combined with the numerous reports of supernatural occurrences, continue to draw paranormal enthusiasts and curious visitors alike, all eager to catch a glimpse of the ghostly inhabitants of this infamous townhouse.

Theories and explanations for the hauntings

THE HOUSE OF DEATH in Greenwich Village, New York, is one of the most infamous haunted houses in the United States. With a long history of supernatural activity and a reputation for being the home to numerous ghosts, the House of Death has been a fascination for ghost hunters and paranormal enthusiasts for decades.

While there are many stories and legends surrounding the house, the cause of the hauntings remains a mystery. However, there are several theories and explanations that have been put forth over the years to try to explain the strange occurrences at the House of Death.

One theory is that the house's dark history and association with the occult have made it a magnet for paranormal activity. The House of Death has been associated with several controversial figures, including Dr. Joel Stein, who practised unconventional and often dangerous medical techniques and had a fascination with the occult. The house was also the home of Jan Bryant Bartell, a self-proclaimed psychic and occultist who wrote about her experiences with the supernatural in the house. Some believe that the negative energy from these past residents has left an imprint on the house and attracted spirits from beyond.

Another theory is that the hauntings at the House of Death are the result of residual energy. Residual energy is the idea that strong emotions or events can leave a lasting impression on a location, which can then be sensed by sensitive individuals. This theory suggests that the traumatic events that occurred in the house, such as the reported suicides and mysterious deaths, have left an imprint on the house, which can be felt by those who visit.

Some paranormal experts have suggested that the hauntings at the House of Death are the result of a portal to the spirit world. A portal is a location where the barrier between our world and the spirit world is said to be thin, allowing spirits to pass through more easily. Some believe that the House of Death is one of these locations and that the high levels of supernatural activity are due to the many spirits passing through.

Others have suggested that the hauntings at the House of Death are simply the result of overactive imaginations. The house's reputation as a haunted site has led many people to expect to experience something supernatural, which may make them more likely to interpret natural phenomena as paranormal. Additionally, the power of suggestion can be a strong force, and many people who visit the house may be influenced by the stories and legends surrounding it.

Despite the many theories and explanations, there is still no conclusive evidence to explain the hauntings at the House of Death. The supernatural activity at the house remains a mystery, and it continues to draw visitors and paranormal investigators from around the world.

Whether you believe in the supernatural or not, the House of Death is a fascinating and eerie location that has captured the imagination of many. With its dark history and numerous reported hauntings, it is easy to see why the house has become one of the most infamous haunted houses in the world.

GHOSTS OF NEW YORK: TEN HAUNTED PLACES IN THE BIG APPLE

93

Chapter 9: The Belasco Theatre

History of the Belasco Theatre

The Belasco Theatre, located at 111 West 44th Street in the heart of Manhattan's Theatre District, is one of the most iconic theatres in New York City. With its ornate Beaux-Arts facade and stunning interior, the Belasco has been a fixture of Broadway since it first opened its doors in 1907.

The theatre was originally built by David Belasco, a legendary figure in the world of theatre who was known for his innovative productions and his dedication to creating immersive, realistic environments for his plays. Belasco was involved in every aspect of the theatre's design, from the facade to the seating arrangement to the intricate lighting system.

One of the most distinctive features of the Belasco Theatre is its use of natural light. Belasco was a pioneer of this technique, which involved using sunlight to create naturalistic effects on stage. To achieve this, he had a massive skylight installed above the stage, as well as a series of movable mirrors that could direct the light onto the actors and set.

Belasco's dedication to realism extended to every aspect of his productions, from the props and costumes to the set design. He was known for his meticulous attention to detail, and he would often spend hours poring over books and historical documents to ensure that every aspect of his productions was historically accurate.

Despite its storied history, the Belasco Theatre has had its share of tragedies over the years. In 1915, a fire broke out in the theatre, causing extensive damage to the stage and auditorium. The theatre was quickly repaired and reopened, but the fire left a lasting mark on the building.

Over the years, the Belasco has been home to many notable productions and performers. In the 1920s, it was the site of the first American production of "Dracula," starring Bela Lugosi. In the 1940s, it was the site of the premiere of Tennessee Williams' "The Glass Menagerie," which went on to become one of the most acclaimed plays of the 20th century.

Today, the Belasco Theatre continues to be a popular venue for Broadway productions. Its stunning interior and rich history make it a favourite among theatre fans and performers alike. In recent years, the theatre has been home to productions such as "Hedwig and the Angry Inch," "A Doll's House, Part 2," and "Network."

Despite its illustrious history, the Belasco Theatre is also rumoured to be haunted. Over the years, many people have reported seeing ghostly apparitions and experiencing strange phenomena inside the theatre.

One of the most commonly reported ghost sightings at the Belasco Theatre is that of David Belasco himself. Some theatregoers and staff members have reported seeing a figure resembling Belasco in the theatre's box seats, dressed in a black suit and bowler hat. Others have reported hearing his distinctive laugh echoing through the building late at night.

Another ghostly presence reported at the Belasco is that of a young woman known as "the Blue Lady." According to legend, the Blue Lady was a former actress who performed at the theatre in the early 20th century. She is said to have died of a broken heart after her lover, a fellow actor, died in a tragic accident on stage. Her ghost is said to haunt the theatre's stage and dressing rooms, and some have reported seeing her ghostly figure dressed in a blue gown.

Despite the many reported sightings of ghosts and supernatural phenomena at the Belasco Theatre, there are no official explanations for the hauntings. Some believe that the theatre's rich history and dramatic past have made it a magnet for supernatural activity, while others believe that the reports of hauntings are simply the result of overactive imaginations.

Whatever the cause of the hauntings may be, the ghostly presence at the Belasco Theatre only adds to the theatre's mystique and allure. The tales of haunted dressing rooms and spectral figures only add to the magic and enchantment of Broadway, drawing in theatre lovers and paranormal enthusiasts alike.

Despite the rumours of hauntings, the Belasco Theatre remains a beloved landmark of Broadway and a testament to the innovative spirit of David Belasco. Its stunning architecture and rich history continue to captivate audiences, and its productions continue to push the boundaries of theatre.

So if you're ever in New York City and looking for a magical night out, be sure to catch a show at the Belasco Theatre. Who knows, you may even catch a glimpse of one of its ghostly inhabitants.

The Ghost of David Belasco

THE BELASCO THEATRE in New York City is one of the most iconic theatres in Broadway, known for its stunning Beaux-Arts facade and rich history. However, the theatre is also famous for its ghostly residents, including the ghost of its founder and namesake, David Belasco.

David Belasco was a legendary figure in the world of theatre, known for his innovative productions and dedication to creating immersive environments for his plays. He was involved in every aspect of the theatre's design, from the facade to the seating arrangement to the intricate lighting system.

Belasco's passion for theatre extended beyond the stage, and it is said that he loved the theatre so much that he never truly left it. After his death in 1931, many people reported seeing his ghostly apparition in the theatre.

The most commonly reported sighting of Belasco's ghost is in the theatre's box seats. He is said to appear dressed in a black suit and bowler hat, watching over the productions that take place on his stage. Many people who have seen his ghostly apparition have reported feeling a sense of awe and reverence, as if they were in the presence of a great artist.

Belasco's ghost is not always visible, but his presence is often felt throughout the theatre. Many people have reported hearing his distinctive laugh echoing through the building late at night, and some have reported smelling his favourite cigar smoke in the air.

The theatre staff has also reported strange occurrences that they believe are caused by Belasco's ghost. Lights have been known to turn on and off by themselves, props and scenery have moved on their own, and the sound of footsteps can be heard when no one else is in the building.

One of the most famous stories involving Belasco's ghost took place in the 1980s, during a production of the musical "La Cage aux Folles." The director, Arthur Laurents, was working late one night in the theatre when he heard someone walking around on the balcony. He assumed it was a member of the staff and called out to them, but there was no response. When he investigated, he found that the balcony was empty.

Later, Laurents was sitting in the theatre's box seats, looking out over the empty stage, when he felt a presence behind him. He turned around and saw the ghostly figure of David Belasco standing behind him, looking over his shoulder. Laurents reported feeling a sense of awe and reverence in the presence of the theatre's founder.

Belasco's ghost has also been known to make appearances during productions. During a performance of "Macbeth" in the 1950s, the actor playing the title role reported feeling a strange presence on stage. When he looked up, he saw the ghostly figure of David Belasco standing in the wings, watching the production.

Despite the many sightings of Belasco's ghost over the years, there are those who remain sceptical. Some believe that the reports of hauntings are simply the result of overactive imaginations or the desire for a good ghost story. Others believe that the strange occurrences at the Belasco Theatre can be explained by natural causes, such as drafts or faulty electrical systems.

However, those who have experienced the presence of Belasco's ghost firsthand believe that there is no explanation other than the supernatural. They believe that the theatre's founder loved the theatre so much that he never truly left it, and that his ghostly presence is a testament to his enduring passion for the art of theatre.

Whether or not you believe in ghosts, there is no denying the rich history and stunning beauty of the Belasco Theatre. Its ornate facade and intricate interior have played host to some of the most acclaimed productions in Broadway history, and its founder's ghostly presence only adds to its mystique. Whether you are a theatre fan, a history buff, or a ghost hunter, the Belasco Theatre is a must-visit destination in the heart of New York City.

Other reported hauntings

WHILE THE GHOST OF David Belasco may be the most well-known spectral resident of the Belasco Theatre in New

York City, there are several other reported hauntings that add to the theatre's eerie reputation.

One of the most commonly reported ghostly presences is that of an actress who is said to have died in the theatre during the early 1900s. Her ghost is said to haunt the stage area, and many people have reported seeing a female apparition wearing a long white dress, walking across the stage or standing in the wings.

The identity of the actress is unknown, but some believe that she may be the ghost of Olive Thomas, a young actress who died in 1920 after ingesting mercury bichloride. Thomas had worked with Belasco and had performed in several plays at the theatre.

Another ghostly presence that is frequently reported is that of a young boy who is said to haunt the balcony area of the theatre. Some believe that he may have been a child actor who performed at the Belasco during the early 1900s and died from an illness.

The boy's ghost is said to be mischievous, and many people have reported feeling their hair or clothing tugged while sitting on the balcony. Others have reported seeing the boy's ghostly figure running up and down the aisles or peeking over the balcony rail.

In addition to these two apparitions, there have been reports of other ghostly sightings and experiences at the Belasco Theatre. Some people have reported feeling a strange presence or sudden cold spots in certain areas of the theatre, while others have reported hearing unexplained noises, such as footsteps or whispers.

One of the most intriguing stories involves a group of actors who were performing a play at the theatre in the 1980s. During one of the performances, the actors reported seeing the ghostly figure of a woman dressed in a long white gown standing in the wings. When they approached her, she disappeared into thin air.

After the show, the actors spoke to the theatre staff about their experience, and it was revealed that no one had been assigned to stand in the wings during the performance. Some believe that the woman in the white gown may have been the ghost of the actress who died in the theatre.

Despite the many reported hauntings at the Belasco Theatre, most people who visit the theatre do not experience any ghostly activity. However, for those who are interested in the paranormal, a visit to the Belasco can be a thrilling and unforgettable experience.

Whether you believe in ghosts or not, the Belasco Theatre's rich history and impressive architecture make it a must-see destination for anyone interested in Broadway theatre. And who knows? You may even catch a glimpse of one of the theatre's spectral residents while you're there.

Theories and explanations for the hauntings

THE BELASCO THEATRE in New York City is known for its ghostly residents, including the ghost of its founder and namesake, David Belasco, as well as several other reported hauntings. While these ghostly sightings and unexplained occurrences are certainly intriguing, there are several theories and explanations that attempt to shed light on these phenomena.

One of the most popular theories is that the hauntings are a result of the intense emotional energy that is created during live theatrical performances. Actors and performers pour their hearts and souls into their performances, creating an emotional energy that can linger long after the show is over. This emotional energy is thought to manifest itself in a variety of ways, including ghostly apparitions, strange sounds, and unexplained movements.

Another theory is that the hauntings at the Belasco Theatre are a result of the building's long and storied history. The theatre has been a fixture of the New York City arts scene since 1907, and has seen countless performances and productions over the years. It is believed that the energy and memories of these past performances have become ingrained in the building itself, creating an environment that is ripe for paranormal activity.

Some people believe that the hauntings at the Belasco Theatre are directly linked to the ghost of David Belasco himself. Belasco was a larger-than-life figure in the world of theatre, and his passion for the art form was said to be unmatched. Some believe that his ghostly presence is simply a reflection of his love for the theatre, and that he continues to watch over the productions that take place on his stage.

Yet another theory is that the hauntings at the Belasco Theatre are simply the result of overactive imaginations. The theatre is a dark and spooky place, with creaky floorboards, musty curtains, and a long history of theatrical performances. It's possible that some people who visit the theatre are already primed to expect ghostly sightings, and their minds may create the paranormal experiences they believe they are having.

However, while these theories and explanations offer some insight into the hauntings at the Belasco Theatre, there is no definitive answer as to why the theatre seems to be a hub of paranormal activity. The truth may lie in a combination of these factors, or it may be something entirely different that we don't yet understand.

Despite the mystery surrounding the hauntings at the Belasco Theatre, one thing is certain: the theatre has become a legendary destination for those interested in the paranormal. Many ghost hunters and enthusiasts have visited the theatre in an attempt to capture evidence of the supernatural, and several paranormal investigation teams have conducted investigations on the premises.

Whether you believe in ghosts or not, there's no denying the allure of the Belasco Theatre and its rich history. The theatre has been the site of countless groundbreaking productions, and its Beaux-Arts facade remains an iconic landmark in New York City. And for those who are interested in the paranormal, the theatre's reported hauntings offer a tantalising glimpse into the unknown.

In the end, the mystery of the Belasco Theatre's hauntings may never be fully solved. But as long as the theatre remains standing, it will continue to captivate the imaginations of theatre lovers, ghost hunters, and curious visitors alike.

Chapter 10: The 9/11 Memorial and Museum

History of the 9/11 Memorial and Museum

The 9/11 Memorial and Museum is a place of remembrance and reflection, honouring the lives lost in the tragic events of September 11, 2001. The memorial and museum, located in lower Manhattan, stands on the site of the former World Trade Center complex, which was destroyed in the terrorist attacks.

The idea for a memorial and museum began shortly after the attacks, as a way to honour the victims and provide a place for people to pay their respects. In 2003, the Lower Manhattan Development Corporation (LMDC) was created to oversee the redevelopment of the World Trade Center site, which included the creation of a memorial and museum.

The LMDC held an international design competition for the memorial, which received over 5,200 entries from 63 countries. The winning design, "Reflecting Absence," was created by Michael Arad, an Israeli-American architect, and Peter Walker, a landscape architect. The design features two large reflecting pools set in the footprints of the former Twin Towers, with water cascading down the sides and into a central void. The names of the victims of the 9/11 attacks, as well as those who died in the 1993 World Trade Center bombing, are inscribed on bronze parapets surrounding the pools.

Construction of the memorial began in 2006, and the memorial was opened to the public on September 11, 2011, the 10th anniversary of the attacks. The memorial quickly became a popular destination for tourists and locals alike, with over 11 million visitors in the first five years after it opened.

In addition to the memorial, plans for a museum to preserve the history and legacy of 9/11 were also in the works. The National September 11 Memorial Museum was designed by the architecture firm Davis Brody Bond, and includes artefacts, personal stories, and interactive exhibits that tell the story of the attacks and their aftermath.

The museum opened to the public on May 21, 2014, and has since become a place of education and remembrance for people from all over the world. Visitors can see artefacts such as twisted steel beams from the World Trade Center towers, a damaged fire truck that responded to the attacks, and a tribute wall filled with personal mementos and messages from loved ones.

The museum also features exhibits that explore the events leading up to the attacks, as well as their impact on the world. One of the most emotional exhibits is the In Memoriam exhibit, which displays photos and personal information about each of the victims of the attacks. Visitors can also hear recordings of the last voicemails and phone calls made by victims to their loved ones, bringing the tragedy and loss to a deeply personal level.

The 9/11 Memorial and Museum is more than just a tourist attraction; it is a place of healing and remembrance for those affected by the attacks. The memorial and museum have played an important role in the healing process for many survivors and families of victims, providing a space to grieve, honour, and remember those who were lost. It serves as a testament to the resilience of the human spirit and a reminder that we must never forget the events of September 11, 2001.

The Ghosts of 9/11 Victims

THE 9/11 MEMORIAL AND Museum in New York City is a place of remembrance and reflection, honouring the victims and heroes of the September 11th terrorist attacks. It is a solemn and respectful space, meant for quiet contemplation and paying tribute to those who lost their lives on that tragic day. However, some visitors to the memorial and museum have reported experiencing paranormal activity, including sightings of ghostly apparitions believed to be the spirits of 9/11 victims.

There have been several reported sightings of ghostly figures at the 9/11 Memorial and Museum. Some visitors have reported seeing the ghostly figures of firefighters or other first responders, walking through the museum as if they were still on duty. Others have reported feeling a sudden drop in temperature or a sudden gust of wind, as if a ghostly presence had passed by them.

One of the most commonly reported sightings at the 9/11 Memorial and Museum is that of a young boy, believed to be the ghost of Jonathan Lee Ielpi. Jonathan was the son of a firefighter who lost his life on 9/11, and he spent many hours at the site of the attacks in the days and weeks that followed. Visitors to the museum have reported seeing the ghostly figure of a young boy playing near the memorial, as if he were reliving his time spent there with his father.

Other visitors to the 9/11 Memorial and Museum have reported feeling a sense of heaviness or oppression, as if the energy in the space is weighing them down. Some have reported feeling dizzy or lightheaded, while others have experienced sudden headaches or other physical discomforts. These sensations are often attributed to the intense emotional energy that is present in the space, as well as the trauma that is associated with the events of 9/11.

While some may dismiss these ghostly sightings and experiences as mere figments of the imagination, others believe that they are a very real and tangible reminder of the profound impact that 9/11 had on the world. The events of that day were so shocking and traumatic that it is not surprising that they would leave a lasting impression on the collective consciousness of those who were affected by them.

The 9/11 Memorial and Museum is a place of deep sorrow and reflection, but it is also a place of hope and resilience. The stories of the victims and heroes of 9/11 continue to inspire and motivate people around the world, reminding us that even in the darkest of times, there is always the possibility of hope and healing. The ghostly presence of those who lost their lives on that tragic day serves as a haunting reminder of the importance of remembering and honouring their memory, and of the need to continue striving for a better and more peaceful world.

Other reported hauntings

THE 9/11 MEMORIAL AND Museum is a powerful and emotional place that pays tribute to the victims of the terrorist attacks that occurred on September 11th, 2001. While the memorial is a place of remembrance and healing for many, there have also been reports of paranormal activity within the museum and surrounding areas.

One of the most commonly reported hauntings at the 9/11 Memorial and Museum is the presence of ghostly apparitions. Many people have reported seeing ghostly figures, both inside the museum and in the surrounding areas, such as Battery Park. These figures are often described as wearing clothing that is consistent with the time period of the attacks, such as business suits or firefighter uniforms.

In addition to ghostly apparitions, there have also been reports of unexplained sounds and movements within the museum. Some visitors have reported hearing the sound of footsteps, even when no one else is around. Others have reported feeling a cold breeze or sudden drop in temperature, despite there being no air conditioning or ventilation in the area.

Another reported haunting at the 9/11 Memorial and Museum is the presence of a young girl who is said to haunt the grounds. According to reports, the girl appears to be around 9 or 10 years old and wears a dress that is reminiscent of the early 20th century. She is often seen playing in the memorial fountains or walking around the grounds. While her identity is unknown, some people believe that she may be a victim of the Triangle Shirtwaist Factory fire, which occurred in 1911.

There have also been reports of hauntings at nearby buildings, such as the Woolworth Building and the St. Paul's Chapel. The Woolworth Building, which is located just a few blocks away from the 9/11 Memorial and Museum, is said to be haunted by the ghost of Frank Woolworth, the building's founder. Some people believe that the ghosts of the 9/11 victims may be drawn to the building because of its historical significance and proximity to the memorial.

Similarly, St. Paul's Chapel, which served as a sanctuary for rescue workers and volunteers in the aftermath of the attacks, has also been the site of reported paranormal activity. Visitors have reported feeling a sense of unease or sadness when inside the chapel, and some have reported seeing ghostly figures or experiencing unexplained movements.

While the reports of hauntings at the 9/11 Memorial and Museum and surrounding areas are certainly intriguing, it's important to approach them with sensitivity and respect. The events of September 11th, 2001, were a tragic and devastating moment in history, and the memorial and museum serve as a powerful reminder of the lives lost and the bravery of the first responders and volunteers who worked tirelessly in the aftermath. Any reported paranormal activity should be viewed in the context of the deep emotional impact of the events of that day, and as a possible reflection of the intense emotions that are still felt by many who visit the site.

Theories and explanations for the hauntings

THE 9/11 MEMORIAL AND Museum in New York City is a place of remembrance, honouring the victims of the tragic events of September 11, 2001. While the memorial and museum are primarily dedicated to preserving the memory of the victims, some visitors and staff members have reported unexplained phenomena that they believe to be related to hauntings.

There are several theories and explanations for the hauntings reported at the 9/11 Memorial and Museum. One theory is that the hauntings are a result of the intense emotional energy that was created during the events of 9/11. The sheer magnitude of the tragedy and the emotions that it evoked may have left an imprint on the site that still lingers today.

Another theory is that the hauntings are a result of the large number of objects that were left behind by the victims and their families. The museum contains thousands of artefacts, from personal belongings to fragments of the buildings themselves. Some believe that the energy of these objects has become infused with the site, leading to paranormal activity.

Additionally, some people believe that the hauntings at the 9/ 11 Memorial and Museum are a result of the spirits of the victims themselves. Many people died suddenly and tragically on 9/11, leaving behind unfinished business and unresolved emotions. It is possible that these spirits are still present at the site, trying to communicate with the living.

There have been numerous reports of ghostly sightings and unexplained phenomena at the 9/11 Memorial and Museum. Visitors have reported seeing apparitions of individuals who perished in the attacks, including firefighters and other first responders. Some have reported hearing the sound of footsteps or voices, despite no one else being present.

In addition to these reported hauntings, there have also been reports of electronic equipment malfunctioning or behaving strangely. Lights have turned on and off by themselves, and some have reported feeling cold spots or sudden changes in temperature.

Despite these reports, it is important to approach the topic of hauntings at the 9/11 Memorial and Museum with respect and sensitivity. The site is a place of remembrance and reverence, and any paranormal activity should be viewed as a possible manifestation of the grief and trauma that occurred there.

The 9/11 Memorial and Museum has taken steps to address these reports of hauntings. They have enlisted the help of paranormal investigators to try and determine the cause of the unexplained phenomena. They have also implemented measures to ensure that visitors and staff members feel safe and comfortable while at the site.

Ultimately, the question of whether the 9/11 Memorial and Museum is haunted remains open to interpretation. While there are many theories and explanations for the reported hauntings, it is up to each individual to decide for themselves what they believe. Regardless of whether one believes in ghosts or not, the site remains a powerful reminder of the tragedy and loss that occurred on September 11, 2001.

Conclusion

New York City is known for many things - bright lights, tall buildings, and a thriving arts scene. However, it's also home to a variety of haunted locations, each with its own unique history and ghostly legends. Let's take a quick look back at the ten haunted places in New York City that we've covered.

The Dakota Building

THIS ICONIC BUILDING is said to be haunted by the ghost of former resident John Lennon, who was tragically murdered outside its entrance. Many people have reported seeing Lennon's ghostly apparition wandering the halls of the building.

The Morris-Jumel Mansion

THIS HISTORIC MANSION in Washington Heights is said to be haunted by the ghost of its former owner, Eliza Jumel. Visitors have reported hearing strange noises and seeing ghostly apparitions throughout the building.

The New Amsterdam Theatre

THIS BROADWAY THEATRE is known for its ghostly residents, including the ghost of Olive Thomas, a former Ziegfeld Follies dancer who is said to haunt the theatre's staircases.

The Empire State Building

WHILE NOT NECESSARILY a haunted location, the Empire State Building is said to be the site of several ghostly sightings, including the ghost of a worker who fell to his death during construction.

The Chelsea Hotel

THIS ICONIC HOTEL HAS been home to many famous residents over the years, including Bob Dylan, Jimi Hendrix, and Andy Warhol. It's also said to be haunted by the ghosts of several former residents, including Dylan Thomas and Nancy Spungen.

The Merchant's House Museum

THIS HISTORIC HOME in Manhattan's East Village is said to be haunted by the ghosts of its former occupants. Visitors have reported strange sounds, ghostly apparitions, and other unexplained occurrences.

The St. Mark's Church-in-the-Bowery

THIS HISTORIC CHURCH is said to be haunted by the ghost of Peter Stuyvesant, the last Dutch governor of New Amsterdam. Visitors have reported seeing his ghostly apparition wandering the church's grounds.

The Belasco Theatre

THIS BROADWAY THEATRE is known for its ghostly residents, including the ghost of its founder and namesake,

David Belasco, as well as several other reported hauntings. The theatre has a long history and is believed to be haunted by the emotional energy created during live theatrical performances, the memories of past productions, and the ghost of David Belasco himself.

The Merchant Marine Academy

THIS MILITARY ACADEMY in Kings Point, Long Island is said to be haunted by the ghost of a former student who committed suicide. Visitors have reported hearing strange noises and feeling a ghostly presence throughout the campus.

The 9/11 Memorial and Museum

THIS SOLEMN SITE IS said to be haunted by the ghosts of the victims of the September 11th terrorist attacks. Visitors have reported feeling a sense of unease and hearing unexplained noises throughout the museum.

While the existence of ghosts and paranormal activity may be a topic of debate, the stories and legends surrounding these haunted places in New York City continue to fascinate and intrigue people. Whether it's the ghost of a famous resident, the energy created during live performances, or the traumatic events of a national tragedy, each location has its own unique history and haunting. For those who are brave enough, visiting these places can be a thrilling and eerie experience, providing a glimpse into the mysterious world of the paranormal.

The idea of hauntings and ghosts has been a topic of interest and fascination for centuries. From classic ghost stories to modern paranormal investigations, the concept of spirits that linger in our world is one that continues to capture our imaginations. But what is the nature of these hauntings and ghosts? Are they real or simply products of our imaginations?

There are many different beliefs and theories about hauntings and ghosts. Some people believe that ghosts are the spirits of the dead who have not yet moved on to the afterlife. They may be stuck in our world for a variety of reasons, such as unfinished business or a traumatic death. These spirits may be searching for closure or trying to communicate with the living.

Others believe that hauntings and ghosts are simply residual energy that has been left behind. This energy may be a result of intense emotions, trauma, or even the physical structure of a building. In some cases, this energy may be strong enough to manifest as ghostly apparitions or other unexplained phenomena.

There are also those who believe that hauntings and ghosts are simply the products of our own minds. These individuals believe that our beliefs, expectations, and imaginations can create experiences that feel very real, but are ultimately the result of our own psychological processes.

Regardless of what you believe, the nature of hauntings and ghosts is a fascinating topic. It raises questions about the afterlife, the human mind, and the power of belief. Whether or not ghosts really exist, the stories and legends that surround them have become an important part of our culture and folklore.

GHOSTS OF NEW YORK: TEN HAUNTED PLACES IN THE BIG APPLE

One thing that is clear is that the concept of hauntings and ghosts has been a source of comfort and healing for many people throughout history. Belief in an afterlife or in the possibility of communicating with the dead can provide a sense of hope and closure for those who have lost loved ones. It can also serve as a reminder that even in death, our spirits may live on in some way.

However, there are also those who have been deeply affected by negative or frightening encounters with ghosts and hauntings. These experiences can be traumatic and leave lasting psychological effects on individuals. It's important to approach the topic with sensitivity and respect for those who may have had negative experiences.

Scientific investigations into hauntings and ghosts have been ongoing for many years, but conclusive evidence has yet to be found. Some researchers have used tools such as electromagnetic field detectors and infrared cameras to try to capture evidence of paranormal activity. Others have studied the psychology behind ghostly experiences, such as the power of suggestion and the role of memory.

Despite the lack of conclusive evidence, the popularity of paranormal investigation shows and the abundance of ghost stories and legends suggest that the fascination with hauntings and ghosts will continue for years to come. Whether you believe in their existence or not, there's no denying the impact that these stories have on our culture and our imaginations.

As we come to the end of our journey through the haunted places of New York City and the nature of hauntings and ghosts, it's important to reflect on what we've learned and gained from this exploration.

First and foremost, we've gained a deeper appreciation for the history and culture of New York City. Each of the haunted locations we've explored has a rich history and a unique story to tell. By learning about these places and the legends that surround them, we've gained a better understanding of the people and events that have shaped this city over the centuries.

Secondly, we've gained a new perspective on the nature of hauntings and ghosts. While there is no definitive proof that ghosts exist, the stories and legends that surround them are a powerful testament to the human imagination and our fascination with the unknown. Whether or not ghosts are real, the experiences and beliefs that surround them are a fascinating part of our cultural heritage.

Finally, we've gained a new appreciation for the power of storytelling. The stories and legends that surround the haunted places of New York City have been passed down through generations, each adding their own unique spin to the tale. By exploring these stories, we've gained a deeper understanding of the power of storytelling to shape our perceptions and beliefs.

Our exploration of the haunted places of New York City and the nature of hauntings and ghosts has been a fascinating and enlightening journey. By learning about these places and the stories that surround them, we've gained a new appreciation for the history and culture of this great city. And by exploring the nature of hauntings and ghosts, we've gained a new perspective on the power of the human imagination and the importance of storytelling in shaping our perceptions and beliefs.

While we may never know for sure whether ghosts really exist, the stories and legends that surround them will continue to capture our imaginations and inspire us for generations to come.

Don't miss out!

Visit the website below and you can sign up to receive emails whenever Edward Turner publishes a new book. There's no charge and no obligation.

https://books2read.com/r/B-A-SYIZ-ESKLC

BOOKS2READ

Connecting independent readers to independent writers.

Also by Edward Turner

Ghosts of Paris: Ten Haunted Places in the City of Love
Ghosts of London: Ten Haunted Places in The City
Ghosts of New York: Ten Haunted Places in The Big Apple

About the Author

Edward Turner is a renowned author who specializes in exploring the realms of ghosts, the paranormal, and cryptids. With a captivating writing style and an insatiable curiosity for the unknown, Turner has garnered a dedicated following of readers who are captivated by his thrilling and eerie tales.

Born with an innate fascination for the supernatural, Turner has spent decades delving into the depths of paranormal phenomena, unearthing captivating stories and untangling mysteries that lie beyond the veil of the ordinary. His extensive research and meticulous attention to detail have earned him a reputation as a leading authority in the field.

Through his books, Turner expertly weaves together chilling accounts of encounters with ghosts, offering readers a glimpse into the ethereal world that coexists alongside our own. His ability to paint vivid portraits of spectral apparitions and convey the haunting atmosphere of haunted locations has made his works both spine-tingling and thought-provoking.

Turner's exploration of the paranormal doesn't stop at ghosts. He also dives into the fascinating world of cryptids—creatures that defy conventional explanation. His in-depth investigations into legendary creatures such as Bigfoot, the Loch Ness Monster, and the Chupacabra showcase his commitment to shedding light on these enigmatic beings.

With each page, Edward Turner's readers are drawn deeper into the enigmatic and unknown. His unique storytelling ability combined with his meticulous research has made him a sought-after author for those with an insatiable thirst for the supernatural. Whether delving into ghostly encounters or unraveling the mysteries of elusive cryptids, Turner's books offer a spine-chilling and immersive reading experience that leaves readers questioning the boundaries of our reality.

Edward Turner's works have earned critical acclaim and numerous accolades within the paranormal genre. He continues to explore the unexplained, captivating readers with his distinctive narrative style and unwavering dedication to unveiling the mysteries that lie hidden in the shadows.